BACKPACKER'S SCOTLAND

Cameron McNeish

ROBERT HALE · LONDON

First published in Great Britain 1982
© *Cameron McNeish 1982*

Robert Hale Limited
Clerkenwell House
Clerkenwell Green
London EC1R 0HT

ISBN 0 7091 9878 7

Photoset in North Wales by
Derek Doyle & Associates, Mold, Clwyd.
Printed in Great Britain by
St Edmundsbury Press, Bury St Edmunds, Suffolk,
and bound by Hunter & Foulis Limited.

Contents

Illustrations

Loch Achray and Ben Venue
Rob Roy's grave in Balquhidder churchyard
St Kessog's Church, the Trossachs kirk
The bleak Mam na Cloich Airde
Loch an Dubh Lochain from Mam Barrisdale
Loch Hourn

Between pages 144 and 145

On the Trotternish Ridge in Skye
The Storr Rock on the Trotternish peninsula
Blair Castle: the beginning of Comyn's Road
On Comyn's Road, leaving the Whim Plantation
Gaick Lodge
Ruthven Barracks: the culmination point of Comyn's Road
An Teallach from the Destitution Road
Beinn Dearg Mhor from Shenavall Bothy
Lord Berkeley's Seat appears through the gloom
On the ridge of Beinn Tarsuinn
Beinn a'Chlaidheimh, Sgurr Ban and Mullach Coire Mhic
  Fhearchair from Beinn Tarsuinn
Looking west over the Great Wilderness from A'Mhaighdean
Winter walker

MAPS

Maps based upon the Ordnance Survey map with the permission of the controller of Her Majesty's Stationary Office. Crown Copyright Reserved.

Dedicated to my father, who put me in the right direction

I hastened to prepare my pack, and tackle the steep ascent that lay before me, but I had something on my mind. It was only a fancy; yet a fancy will sometimes be importunate. I had been most hospitably received and punctually served in my green caravanserai. The room was airy, the water excellent, and the dawn had called me to a moment. I say nothing of the tapestries or the inimitable ceiling, nor yet of the view which I commanded from the windows; but I felt I was in someone's debt for all this liberal entertainment. And so it pleased me, in a half laughing way, to leave pieces of money on the turf as I went along, until I had left enough for my night's lodgings.

Travels with a Donkey
Robert Louis Stevenson

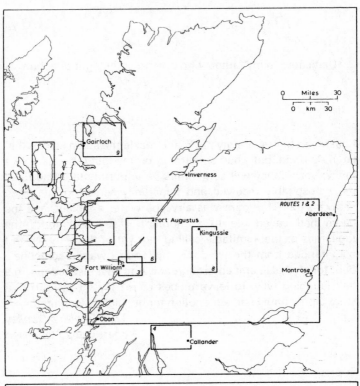

Key to maps 3-9

Route of walk	– – – – –	Peak (with height)	▲ *(3173')*
Main road		Youth hostel	*
Minor road		Building	■

Introduction

Morna, fairest among women,
A stream murmurs by the side,
An aged tree whistles in the wind;
Yonder lake is troubled by the gale,
Black clouds surround the top of the hills,
But thou art like snow on the heath,
Thy ringlets are like the mists of Cromla,
When it climbs the side of the hill,
In the beams of the Western sun.

The words of Ossian, bardic son of the mighty warrior Fingal, whose legends and deeds are recorded even today in place-names of glens, corries, mountain tops and lochsides throughout the Scottish Highlands. This is the real romance and nostalgia of Scotland; the Celtic love of a homeland, passed down from father to son from time immemorial. The tales and legends of Scotland, in all their life, in all their mystery, in all their beauty, can strike a chord in the hearts of all those who love the wild and lonely places of the Highlands.

Scotland provides a rich tapestry for the backpacker, a fabric woven from the threads of experiences, senses and impressions; the sound of a curlew, the tangle of wind on an upturned face, the scents of damp earth and bog myrtle, the challenge of the upward strive, the discovery of secret corners lost in silent glens. To search for these experiences, to find these hidden places, to look for a country undefiled, is to forsake all easy roads and travel by twisting hill tracks, to forsake a soft bed and a served breakfast and travel with one's belongings contained in a rucksack, carried by the fortitude of one's own sweat.

It was the romance and mystery of the Highlands which first inspired me to climb mountains and stravaig the quieter, wilder highways of Scotland, and even after almost twenty years I am still fascinated by the atmosphere, the colours and impressions, which have never failed to invoke in me a sense of wonder and deep humility.

The Highland weather, so strongly cursed by many and yet so misunderstood, has often provided the stimulation that comes only from being in an environment which is so often enhanced by wreaths of mist or sunlight filtered through a cloud level which, from below, may appear depressing. Many are the occasions when it is a struggle to leave a cosy tent or flickering bothy fire, when the drizzle and cloud seem, at first, impenetrable, only to find that, once the hillside is reached, you are enjoying it in some strange supercilious way. How often that mental struggle is rewarded by a clearing of the cloud, even momentarily, like a curtain being swiftly raised, over a complete landscape that looks as though it has been newly washed and hung out to dry in the fresh breeze. Then there are the days which remain longest in the memory, when the hills are purple and languid in the warm sun, when the lazy call of the cuckoo seems a fitting emblem in the heavy, slumbering atmosphere of the day, when every burn is an oasis, and every far-flung view shimmers on a haze borne by sun on damp rock and heather.

Perhaps the prime factor that makes Scotland so different is that once, and not so very long ago, the wild areas were inhabited. As the passage of history records, the clan system and ethnic cultures were cruelly desecrated by man's misunderstanding and greed, so much of the song and story which remains reminds us of the grief and sorrow of the forced emigrant. The tall ships in the bay, awaiting the transportation of their human cargos to the new colonies; the evicted families, clinging to their meagre possessions and trying in vain to wrest a survival from the wind-scoured shore; the burnt-out shells which were once their homes. These ruins remain, to remind us that men and women once tended their cattle here in the summer shielings. Now there is just the wind, and the occasional tread of walkers enjoying the stark beauty that inspired a folklore of song and pibroch.

I have selected nine walks varying greatly in degree of difficulty and in distance. None of the chosen walks is an official long-distance footpath, a foreign animal which is totally unnecessary in a country where access is free, apart from the deer-stalking and grouse-shooting seasons. In most areas deer stalking begins in early September, but officially from 20th July. It goes on until 20th October, although hind culling continues until February. With the exception of certain marked areas, it is not always difficult to gain access during the hind cull. From the Glorious Twelfth, 12th August, grouse shooting can affect lower levels and access. The golden rule is, if in doubt, ask locally.

Finally, a word on the format of the book. The brief itineraries at the beginning of each route, and in some cases interspersed throughout the route description, are not, in any way, meant to be a substitute for a map. They are there as a quick reference to be traced on the appropriate Ordnance Survey map. The route descriptions offer my experiences and feelings on the route, as well as attempting to describe the physical terrain which the route covers, as well as some of the pertinent history of the areas passed through. The folklore of old is a powerful motivation to experience the winds and whispers of one's homeland, and the man who knows something of the history of his chosen place of wandering can share in the ultimate triumph of the outdoors: the sense of belonging that is experienced long before familiarity breeds the pretentiousness of believing that you know the place.

> Beloved is that land, Alba with its lakes,
> Oh that I might not depart from it,
> Unless I were to go with Naoise,
> Oh that I might not leave this land,
> Unless it were to come along with me – Beloved.

Dan Chloinn Uisheachain

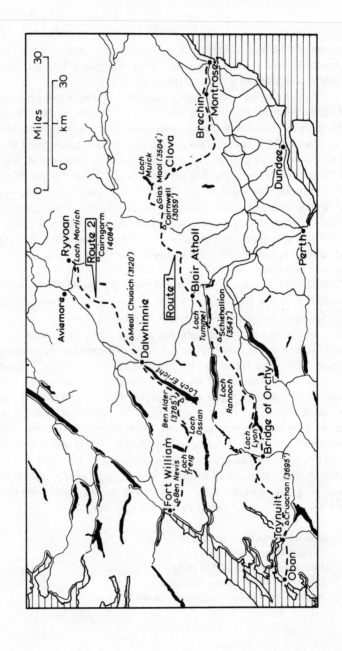

ROUTE 1: TRANS-SCOTLAND WALK: OBAN TO MONTROSE

About 208 miles. An eight-camp trans-Scotland walk over mixed terrain, taking in 20 Munros.

Maps required: O.S. 1:50,000 Second Series. Sheets 49, 50, 51, 43, 44, 54.

(There are many alternatives which can be chosen on this route, to avoid mountain tops, by judicious map planning.)

Leave the Esplanade in Oban by walking south down George Street to Argyll Square, then S.E. by Combie Street for 200 yards before turning left at the Parish Church into Glencruitten Road. Follow this road to the golf links, then through the tunnel under the railway line and into Glen Lonan. Follow the road through Glen Lonan to Taynuilt. Leave Taynuilt eastwards, and follow the A85 for 3 miles to Bridge of Awe. Cross the bridge, take minor road north for 100 yards, cross the railway bridge and strike N.E. up steep slopes of Ben Cruachan beside the Allt Cruiniche. Climb up to bealach between Meall nan Each and the 1100-metre top of Cruachan, and then ascend the latter from the high point of the bealach. Follow the obvious ridge of Ben Cruachan eastwards, over the 3695 foot summit to Stob Diamh, 3272 feet. Drop down north ridge of Stob Diamh to Coire Lochain. Camp. Traverse eastwards from Coire Lochain into Glen Noe, and ascend south ridge of Beinn a'Chochuill, 3215 feet, 1½ miles. Follow curving ridge eastwards for 1 mile, then ascend rocky slopes of Beinn Eunaich, 3242 feet. Walk N.E. on obvious ridge for 1½ miles to Meall Copagach, then descend north ridge into Glen Kinglass, 1½ miles. Ford river to reach north bank, and follow the track N.E. for 6 miles, to Loch Dochard, then due E. for 3¾ miles by Linne nam Beathach to Forest Lodge. From Forest Lodge, cross the Linne nam Beathach by Victoria Bridge and follow the A8005 to bridge over Allt Tolaghan, then swing E. to Inveroran Hotel. Pass hotel, and 100 yards beyond, follow the sign of the West Highland Way, following the track S.E. over the shoulder of Mam Carraigh to Bridge of Orchy, $3\frac{1}{2}$ miles. Cross A82, go through the railway station and strike E. on to the moorland below Coire an Dothaidh. Camp in vicinity.

The Argyllshire town of Oban has always stirred in me happy memories of holidays in the west. Just as the Atlantic winds of Connemara blow through the grey streets of Galway Town, so the atmosphere of the Western Isles begins in mainland Oban. From the arched remnants of McCaig's Folly, high above the town and the blue sheltered bay, the sea ways open out before you; to green Kerrera and beyond, Lismore and Mull, Staffa and Iona, Coll and Tiree, before the islands of the Outer Hebrides herald the edge of the great Atlantic.

It is a lively, bustling town, even at 9 a.m. on a May morning. The railway pier was all a-jostle with herring trawlers and lobster boats, and the wide jaws of the *Columba*, the Mull ferry, were gorging on a steady flow of cars, lorries and vans. The smell of fish and diesel oil, the familiar stench of a fishing port, hung heavily in the salt air, and the gulls swooped and flocked, their cries all but drowning out the steady throb of *Columba*'s engines. Roger Smith and I left our sea-front hotel, and made our way along the Esplanade. Across the bay, the low outline of Kerrera, with the high hills of Mull in the background, unlocked a host of memories; a hotchpotch of past ploys in the Isles whirled through my thoughts. On these trips, Oban had been the starting point of forays to the west; today, I would be turning my back on Oban Bay and looking eastwards, to ten days of walking and climbing which would take us across the breadth of Scotland to Montrose on the east coast. Our walk had been inspired by a challenge by Ultimate Equipment, an outdoors equipment manufacturer, who were hoping to initiate an annual trans-Scotland backpacking event, where walkers would have some planning and advisory backup, and a central point to which they could telephone every couple of days or so to advise of their progress. In this way, walkers who were new to Scotland could walk across the breadth of the country in confidence, knowing that their progress was being monitored, and advice on route finding or potential problems was only a phone call away.

Roger Smith, my companion on this coast-to-coast, is a Londoner by birth, but has lived in Scotland for several years. An orienteer and fell runner of long experience, he immediately fell in love with the Scottish hills when he moved north, and was relentlessly ticking off the Munros, the Scottish hills over 3000 feet, at a cracking pace. Our coast-to-coast would give him several new ones for his collection, and I looked forward to showing him the great variety of scenery that Scotland has to offer on a trip of this kind. With my backpacking and camping experience I was elected chief cook and bottle washer; Roger, an an orienteer, was given the perplexing job of navigator. His first task was to get us out of Oban.

Rather than risk death with the cars and lorries on the busy A85 Oban to Taynuilt road, we chose a quieter route of 12 miles through Glen Lonan to the Etiveside village of Taynuilt, from where we would have 3 miles of walking on the main road before leaving it for the steep slopes of Cruachan Beinn, or as it is on the O.S. 1:50,000 map, Ben Cruachan. We left the noises and smells of the sea front behind us, and walked south through the town, past rows of hotels and guest houses bracing themselves for the annual tourist influx, and on to the long pull out of town past the golf course. Although it was only early May, the trees and bushes were in full flower, the yellow on the broom contrasting vividly with the pale green of birch, oak and alder. This is a rich landscape, as much of Lorne is, and it must have seemed a great attraction to the Irish priests who landed here from Ireland all those hundreds of years ago, to preach, and convert the druidic Picts.

Glen Lonan offered us an almost ideal start to our long journey, past the shinty stadium and the golf course, below the old railway bridge, and a long climb through oak trees before the road wound gently down into the actual glen. Gulls shrieked and yelled in and above Loch Nell, swooping and diving in raucous abandon. The sounds of spring were around us: the thrumming of snipe, the warbled fluting of a curlew, the vibrant shrillness of a skylark, and my first cuckoo of the year!

The glen narrows considerably in places, the hills on either side rising up to more than 2000 feet. The river too widens and narrows as it makes its way through the valley, and today it was alive with the bustle of dippers. We passed through woods of pine, the resinous scent strong in the mild air, then over wide stretches of moor, heavy with the fragrance of a thousand honeyed scents, where the road seemed to wander at will, sometimes up, sometimes down, until at last, with the waters of Loch Etive glinting in the distance, surrounded by high mountains, we emerged from the glen into Taynuilt.

It was lunchtime, and we had just walked on to Sheet 50 of the O.S. 1:50,000 map series. The 12 miles from Oban, although very pleasant, had been hard on the feet, and they were feeling a little battered by the unforgiving tarmac. We took the opportunity of cooling off for half an hour in the public bar of the hotel and, over a couple of pints of quenching shandy, we planned our afternoon. Between Taynuilt and where we hoped to camp for the night, frowned the great rocky barrier of Ben Cruachan, the Mountain of Peaks, whose great slopes presented us with a climb from more or less sea level, to over three and a half thousand feet. We had set ourselves a hefty day, about 20 miles of walking with four to five thousand feet of climbing, but we felt fit enough to manage it. Later on in the afternoon we weren't quite so cheekily confident.

Leaving the village, we were joined by a happy gaggle of schoolchildren going off home for lunch, making us feel a bit like overburdened Pied Pipers! The long swell and sharp peak of Cruachan's Taynuilt Peak rose up in front of us, its summit just decapitated by cloud. Heads down, packs creaking, we battered on, desperate now to get off the hard tarmac as soon as possible, even though we would be exchanging the flat road for a steep-sided mountain flank! Bridge of Awe came not a minute too soon, and crossing the bridge over the railway, we immediately began to climb the lower bracken-covered slopes of Cruachan.

The normal route of ascent of Cruachan is by way of the stream which flows from the hydro-electric reservoir high in the south-facing corrie above the Pass of Brander, a few miles further east. This route has the advantage of a bulldozed track up to the level of the reservoir, about 1300 feet above sea level, but our route, via Cruachan's most westerly top, climbs trackless all the way from sea level. We unhesitatingly voted, nevertheless, that a track to 1300 feet was not worth the miseries of another 4 miles of foot pounding and lorry dodging on the busy road. The tumbling Allt Cruiniche led us up the steep slopes to a boggy bealach between the outlying Meall nan Each and Stob Dearg, the western peak of Cruachan, which is commonly referred to as the Taynuilt Peak. It was W.P. Ker, the poet, who, perhaps in a state of chronic homesickness, once referred to the Nordend of Monte Rosa as its Taynuilt Peak.

Above us, a steep ridge leads into the black clouds. We changed from shorts into breeches, and put our waterproof jackets on. It was like changing from spring back into winter. The mild freshness of Glen Lonan had evaporated into cold and damp, and things began to look a bit forlorn. We were both in the first throes of tiredness, and the misplaced enthusiasm of the morning had been replaced by a more realistic realization of what we had set for ourselves the first day out. Very quickly, it became obvious that we were heading into a dangerous situation. Long greasy slabs of wet rock lay at a steep angle, and the gullies in between were choked with wet slobbery snow. Several times I led the way up promising-looking clefts between the slabs, and each time I had to climb back down again delicately. The weight in my pack pulled me backwards, and my legs felt like rubber after their 15-mile hammering on the roads. Roger seemed to have lost his bouncy optimism, and we began seriously to consider a retreat to the bealach where we could spend the night. A small lochan would provide water, and several flat spots looked as though they would be sheltered enough. It was now almost 4.30 p.m., and it was still a long way over Cruachan. Rather than drop down immediately, we began traversing around the slope to the north, when, completely unexpectedly, I stumbled over what was an obvious path. It was intermittent, but it was an obvious route to the top. All thoughts of an early camp now gone, we scrambled up loose scree, sliding backwards almost as much as we climbed, over some blocks of rough granite, and suddenly we were on top beside the cairn. Smiles replaced worried frowns, limp limbs felt strong again, and a steepish drop, a long level ridge, and another short clamber over boulders had us on the actual summit of Ben Cruachan by 5.30 p.m., 3695 feet above sea level. As I sat by the cairn digging into my pack for something to eat, a cry from Roger made me look up. The dark cloud which had been billowing around us suddenly lifted like some giant curtain, and the view which opened up before us was as breathtaking as it had been sudden. Below, the Cruachan reservoir filled the contours of the corrie floor; Loch Awe stretched its long arm south-west, the longest loch in Scotland, and away beyond, the island-speckled sea led to the hazy west. Eastwards, the ridge opened out in a series of bumps and dips and peaks, more like a small range of mountains than one single hill. To the north, the Blackmount and Glencoe tops appeared in a jumble, and away eastwards, beyond the end of Cruachan, the familiar fine shape of Ben Lui rose high from its lower neighbours.

We left the cairn, jubilant now that the weather was showing a kind face to us. It certainly helped us stagger along the ridge towards Stob Daimh, Cruachan's second Munro at 3272 feet. We still felt very, very tired, and if a pool of water or a stream had appeared in front of us, I think we would have thankfully camped there and then, despite the exposed elevation of over 3000 feet.

Coming off the summit of Cruachan, the ridge flows east and then slightly north-east, over the uncairned top of Drochaid Glas, 3312 feet. This is a narrow rocky top, and in mist or cloud it would be all too easy to carry on down the steep and narrow north ridge into Glen Noe. The ridge to Stob Daimh in fact is best reached by dropping down about 20 yards short of Drochaid Glas, and on to the north-east ridge, which descends, levels out, and then climbs again to Cruachan's second Munro.

Stob Daimh greeted us with sunshine and good views of our hills for the next day, Beinn a'Chochuill and Beinn Eunaich, a lofty pair lying to the north-east across the void of the Bealach Noe. Below our feet, in its own scooped out corrie, a small lochan glinted blue, reflecting the now clear skies above. We looked at each other, and without speaking, started off down the north ridge into the corrie. Words weren't necessary, it was the obvious place for a camp; shelter, water, and what promised to be a fine view with a sunset thrown in for good measure. It turned out to be, in fact, a delectable campsite, and we both awarded it five stars.

I pitched the tent on a grassy shelf, while Roger collected water from the lochan. The first cup of tea laced with lemon was simply glorious, the second even better. Then came the food; pea and ham soup, macaroni and cheese, spicy beef and mashed potato, more tea, and coffee to finish. To add the splendid finishing touch Roger produced a small flask of whisky from his pack, and we lay outside and sipped it luxuriously, as we watched a crimson sunset over the Glen Etive hills. As the sky above us grew darker, and the first stars began to appear in the velvet blackness, we slipped inside and into our sleeping bags; tired, bone sore, but extremely satisfied with our first day out.

Morning came almost too soon, but it was sunny, with only the tops wreathed in a thin delicate mist. We didn't waste time; a quick breakfast, pack up, and we were off, traversing eastwards around the rough slabby ridge and down on to the

Bealach Noe which separates Cruachan from Beinn a'Chochuill. A prominent ridge drops down to the bealach from the summit of Chochuill, and we went straight up it. It was steep, and prolonged, but we managed to reach the summit cairn inside 40 minutes, to flop down beside the cairn and enjoy the views across to the shapely peaks of Cruachan we had traversed the night before.

Beinn a'Chochuill is the Peak of the Hood, and it is linked to Beinn Eunaich by a long bow-shaped ridge. A huge snow cornice still decorated the north side of the ridge, and we sludged across a couple of runny snow fields on the slopes of Eunaich. We were on the summit by 10.30 a.m., our two Munros for the day gone, and only a long easy walk on tracks and paths for the rest of the day; almost a holiday by yesterday's standards.

A north-east ridge runs from Eunaich to Meall Copagach, green, broad and wide. We followed it for about $1\frac{1}{2}$ miles, then dropped down the bracken-covered flanks into Glen Kinglass, a particularly charming glen which runs from Ardmaddy on Loch Etiveside to Loch Dochard, near Bridge of Orchy. Deep bracken covered the river banks, and pine, birch and alder formed a natural archway over the river itself, which rushed refreshingly through a succession of deep, clear pools. We were hot and sweaty after our quick descent, and were easily seduced by the delights of the glen; a bathe and a picnic lunch could not be resisted. As we lay back in the hot sun, stripped to our underpants, our feet sizzling in the cool water, it wasn't difficult to convince ourselves that this was what backpacking was all about, lazing around enjoying the pleasures of life.

After an hour we were back in harness again. The walk was simply magnificent. The great hills of the Blackmount Forest shimmered in the heat as we followed the superb path over its high pass and down towards Loch Dochard. Away in front of us the Bridge of Orchy hills, Beinn an Dothaidh and Beinn Dorain, towered high, the high pass between them our route for the morning. Forest Lodge came and went in a haze of blazing heat, the starting point of many previous trips into Blackmount. We crossed Victoria Bridge, a nineteenth-century arch over the Linne nam Beathach and, shortly after that, passed an old track which runs off in a south-westerly direction. If you have time, wander along it for a mile or so, because in Gleann Fuar, a pile of rubble and stones lies as a sad monument to one of Scotland's greatest poets. Duncan Ban MacIntyre was born here in 1724, and he eventually became the greatest of all the Gaelic bards. His works were composed entirely in his mother tongue, the Gaelic, and this is probably the reason he did not gain the recognition he deserved. Duncan could not read, nor write, as schooling was practically non-existent in these rural areas in his day, but his works were composed and committed totally to memory, usually as he wandered around the hills of Beinn Dorain or Buachaille Etive Mor as gamekeeper, later to be promoted under-forester, to the Earl of Breadalbane. His works have been handed down by other Gaelic scholars throughout the years, and many have been documented and enjoyed by thousands of Gaelic speakers the world over.

We didn't visit the birthplace of Donachadh Ban nan Oran, or Fair Haired Duncan of the Songs, as he was known, as the combination of heat and a dusty trail had given us gargantuan thirsts, and since it was less than a mile to one of the finest hostelries in the country, the Inveroran Hotel by Loch Tulla, we didn't linger. This establishment crouches amidst a fine clutch of pines at the south-western corner of Loch Tulla, and is a link with the old coaching days when a service ran from Glasgow to Fort William. The Wordsworths stopped here on their way south from Kingshouse during their Highland jaunt, but they were not impressed: "The butter not eatable, the barley cakes fusty, the oatbread so hard I could not chew it, and there were only four eggs in the house which they boiled as hard as stones." To be fair to the Inveroran, the Wordsworths did have to share the inn with a gaggle of drovers who had just been fed, so perhaps they were lucky to get anything to eat at all!

Many is the time I have limped into the Inveroran, hot and

tired, and more often, cold, wet and wind-battered, and always I have experienced the most excellent and friendly service. Today, alas, the Inveroran let me down, but it was not their fault, more the fault of the Scottish laws on drinking alcohol on a Sunday. The bar wouldn't be open until six, and it was only just going on five. We had a decision to make; batter on over to Bridge of Orchy with our tongues hanging out like exercised dogs, or stop beside Inveroran for an hour, no hardship in the still sweltering sun, to await the serving of cooling liquor. Our intention was to camp as near as dammit to the high pass which runs between Beinn Dothaidh and Beinn Dorain to Glen Lyon, and that was still 4 miles and about 2000 feet of climbing away. While we did not particularly mind pushing our body to further levels of tiredness, though at that time the spirit was rather weak, we pushed on, not wanting to waste any time. That eventually turned out to be the wrong decision.

Rather than walk around the roads by the woods of Coire Darach, we followed the old military road which cuts off the bend in the road, by climbing over the high shoulder of Mam Carraigh. This is part of the Glasgow to Fort William West Highland Way, Scotland's first official long-distance footpath, a totally unnecessary creation whose setting up caused a furore. In a country like Scotland where access is unrestricted, it seems a strange policy to concentrate walkers in a narrow ribbon of track, and this particular section, less than a year after its opening, is already showing severe signs of erosion. We walked over the shoulder wallowing in ankle-deep glutinous mud, and it was clear by the unnatural width of the track that West Highland Way pedestrians were already spreading out on this part of the track, actually widening the effects of the erosion. We felt a bit deflated as we slithered and slid our way down towards Bridge of Orchy. We were depressed by the mess of the track, and our mood was blackened even further as we stood in the bar of the hotel, trying our best to avoid listening to the drunken rantings of some football supporters on their way home from the Scottish Cup Final in Glasgow. We quickly drank up and left, saddened by our brush with civilization. Outside, the cloud was now building up quickly, and any hopes of another sunset were diminishing rapidly. Up through the railway station we went, through the gate on to the open hillside, and up towards our bealach gateway to Glen Lyon. We stopped at the first suitable pitch we found, and a good one it was; a flat ledge of grass in a rocky depression beside the river. After a quick supper, we turned in, burnt and weary, our thoughts turning towards the long section we had planned for the next day.

Ascend slopes of Coire an Dothaidh and through the high pass between Beinn an Dothaidh and Beinn Dorain. Follow the Allt Coire a'Ghabhalach eastwards to its confluence with the Allt Chonoghlais, then walk due E. on good footpath to Loch Lyon. 4 miles. Follow the north shore of Loch Lyon for 7 miles to the dam at its head, then follow tarmac road for 10 miles past Cashlie, Stronuich, Meggernie, Bridge of Balgie to Innerwick. Camp in vicinity of Innerwick. Ascend S.W. slopes of Beinn Dearg to summit plateau, $1\frac{1}{4}$ miles, then descend N.E. to bealach between Beinn Dearg and Carn Gorm. Ascend eastwards to Carn Gorm, 3370 feet, 2 miles. Follow broad N.E. ridge to Meall Garbh, 3150 feet, $1\frac{1}{4}$ miles, then due E. for $1\frac{1}{2}$ miles to N.W. top of Carn Mairg. Leave pack, and ascend over rocky slopes (not shown on map) to summit of Cairn Mairg, 3419 feet, $\frac{1}{2}$ mile. Return and collect pack, and follow broad N. ridge to Meallanan Odhar, then N.E. to broad bealach between Geal Charn and Schiehallion, $2\frac{1}{4}$ miles. Ascend Schiehallion by its W.N.W. slopes, then descend by path E., for 1 mile, then N.E. to Braes of Foss, 4 miles. Walk N.N.E., passing to the W. of Craig Kynachan, and drop down slopes to Tummel Bridge. Commercial campsite or BB.

Billowing storm clouds and a strong southerly breeze greeted us in the morning, greyly obliterating any views we may have looked forward to. Today was to be a 20-mile plus one, 10 miles on rough track, and 10 on unyielding tarmac, but our packs were the lightest they had been since we left Oban; we carried little food now, relying on a cache which Roger had dumped a couple of weeks before at Innerwick in Glen Lyon.

A rough path climbs up into Coire an Dothaidh, but soon vanishes in amongst the rocks and crags which fringe the top of this high bealach. We climbed up quietly, both of us a little depressed by the grey world we had wakened up to, but, as we crossed the pass, it was almost as though we were walking into a different world. The sun momentarily glanced through from between scudding clouds, casting vast beams of gold on the brilliant greenery of the hills around us. The slopes were alive with spring, golden plovers were calling and the incessant twee-twee of pipits intermingled with the chorus of bleating lambs and sheep. We followed the wren-loud burn, the Allt Coire a'Ghabhalach, down to its confluence with the Allt Chonoghlais, a place teeming and stinking with the sounds and smells of sheep. A short distance south of here, a ruined shieling stands empty and forlorn, nowadays used as a sheep pen. This was once the shepherds' house of t-Sithein, where Duncan Ban MacIntyre lived when he was under-forester in the employ of the Earl of Breadalbane. Today, the ruins are caked in sheep dung, and the stench of the place assaults your nostrils even from several hundred yards off, a cruel twist of irony, for Fair Haired Duncan, like many of his ilk, blamed the introduction of sheep farming for the fall of the old clan patriarchal system, the beginning of the downfall of the Highland way of life, and he had a real and intense loathing for the creatures. This hatred is explained in one of his poems, "Oran Nam Balgairean", the Song of the Foxes, as is his apparent sympathy with the anathematized fox;

> My blessing be upon the foxes, because that they hunt the sheep,
> The sheep with the brockit faces that have made confusion in all
> the world,
> Turning our country to desert and putting up the rents of our lands,
> Now is no place left for the farmer – his livelihood is gone;
> Hard necessity drives him to forsake the home of his fathers,
> The townships and the shielings, where once hospitality dwelt,
> They are now nought but ruins, and there is not cultivation in the
> fields.

There is no filly, no mare with foal by her side,
Gone too are the heifers which suckled their calves,
No need is there of dairymaids, for every fold is broken and
:   scattered,
No lad can earn a wage, save only the shepherd of the sheep.

Deeply do I hate the men who abuses the foxes,
Setting a dog to hunt them, shooting at them with small shot,
The cubs, if they had what I wish them, short lives were not their
                                                    care,
Good luck to them say I, and may they never die but of old age.

By some weird coincidence, as we wandered along the track
which leads to Loch Lyon beside the Allt a'Chuirn, I almost
tripped over what I thought at first was a sleeping dog. It was a
dead fox, lying there in the middle of the track, its long brush
tail stretched out behind it. It hadn't been dead all that long by
the looks of it, as the gulls, crows and raven hadn't been at it,
but it was an odd find. It was a big dog fox, probably old
judging from the amount of grey around its muzzle. Perhaps it
just lay down here to die, or perhaps it was the victim of some
poison which had been laid for it. We will never know.

A line of fishermen stood at the head of Loch Lyon, the wind
gusting down the long empty miles of the loch roughing the
waters into a cavalry charge of white horses. A right of way
exists alongside the north shore of the loch, but for the first 4
miles there is no path or track. The brief interlude of golden sun
had gone, and in its place a grey melancholy haze had settled.
The cloud base was still high, well above the summits of the
Mamlorn Hills to our south, but the hills themselves appeared
blank and featureless silhouettes in that enveloping veil of
haze, and in front of us, our shoreline led onwards over the dull
slopes of Beinn Mhanach in an equally dull-looking trudge. It
quickly became frustrating walking; we tried walking higher up
the hillside, but the deep heather made the going very
uncomfortable; we tried walking on the shore of the loch but
the soft sand and gravel made it slow laborious going. In the

end we struck a compromise and stravaiged from shore to slope to suit the underfoot conditions of the time. My log at the time describes the frustrations: "Loch Lyon side hellish. Walking across a steep angle on ancient sheep tracks; when we were lucky!! Very hard work, down into, and back out of endless gullies, weather closing in again, wind in our face. A bit grim."

All we could do was frown and bear it, as the long empty miles struggled by, around the awkward indent of the loch, where our impatience to get around tempted us into wading across a stretch of black oozy mud, rather than walking all the way around the shoreline. During these harassing miles we walked off Sheet 50 of the O.S. 1:50,000 Second Series, and onto Sheet 51.

It was 1 p.m. by the time we reached the path which would take us the remaining 3 miles along Loch Lyon to the road at Pubil. It was during these rather unpleasant hours that I appreciated the wisdom of selecting a walking partner with similar attitudes to one's own, if one must take a partner along at all. Roger and I had walked in silence, both of us suffering inwardly. What's the point of complaining loudly? We were both well aware of the job to be done, so we just buckled down and got on with it. Whilst suffering alone, we suffered together, quietly, and that type of sharing creates firmer friendships than the easier sharing of happy things.

We treated ourselves to a long lunch by a stream, putting the stove on for a brew, and building ourselves up mentally for the long slog which we knew was before us in the afternoon. We had already come about 9 miles since our night's camp, but we still had to break the back of our day's tally. The 3 remaining miles of the lochside would do that, leaving us with a foot-pounding 10-12 miles on the road down Glen Lyon.

The last 3 miles of lochside walking wasn't pleasant, albeit on a track. The grey cheerless weather made it "gey dreich" walking, the track being comprised of countless up-and-down, in-and-out-of gullies, and finally climbing quite high above the loch before dropping down to the great dam at its head. Loch Lyon is part of a large system of lochs and tunnels which have been harnessed by the Hydro-electric Board, its size having been doubled by being raised from 100 to 170 feet, thus flooding old tracks, roads and houses. Those who were unfortunate enough to lose their homes by the raising of the level of the loch have been accommodated in a new hamlet called Pubil just east of the dam, a dreary-looking huddle of new houses which will never have the character of the buildings which they replaced.

Ahead of us now stretched the road, eastwards, and then gradually curving north-east to Bridge of Balgie and then Innerwick. Glen Lyon is the longest glen in Scotland, winding for some twenty miles from its loch eastwards to Aberfeldy, and it is steeped in history. These upper reaches are traditionally associated with Finn MacCuill, or Fingal, or even Fionn, whose mighty army of Homeric-type heroes, the Fianna, were said to have their homes here in the "duns" and ancient fortresses which are sited at regular intervals along two miles of the River Lyon.

I read a Neil Munro novel, *John Splendid*, as I tramped along the hard jolting miles, Roger walking a short distance off, lost in his own Sunday afternoon thoughts. I was perhaps doing this fine glen an injustice by burrowing my nose in a book, for it is one of the most contrastingly beautiful glens in the Highlands. From the bare remote hills of Loch Lyon it runs alongside high mountain flanks, the desolation spoiled by the intrusions of the Hydro-electric Board, until, after 7 or 8 miles, it sweeps round beside a bend in the river, to become a gentle wooded landscape, the lower hillsides painted in the vibrant colours of Scots pines, sycamores, birches, beeches and oaks. Below the road, by the river, lies the extravagance of Meggernie Castle, at the head of its long avenue of limes. The castle was built in 1593 by Mad Colin Campbell who is said to have made the first recorded ascent of Stuchd an Lochain, the prominent Munro which lies between Loch Lyon and Loch an Daimh to the north. If that wasn't enough to pronounce him mad (only modern man is crazy enough to go walking the hills for fun!) it is claimed that the bold Colin had a bent for driving herds of sheep and goats over the high north-east facing cliffs of the hill, and he truly lived up to his nickname when he tried to do the same thing in one of his ghillies!

As the remaining 3 foot-weary miles to Innerwick crept past, the glen became more enclosed, the foothills of the Lawers range in the south almost encroaching on the southern slopes of the Carn Mairg range which lies between Glen Lyon and Loch Rannoch in the north. A post office is marked on the O.S. map, at Bridge of Balgie, but being a Sunday, it was locked and shuttered. As Roger phoned home from the phone box outside, I peered through the window to see cans of soft drink gaze tantalizingly back at me. With twenty hard miles behind us, that was almost too much to bear!

Innerwick is comprised of a church and a few scattered houses, and it was to one of these that we went to collect the food cache that Roger had previously left in one of his recent forays into the Glen Lyon Hills. There was no answer to our knocks at the door, but we found the parcel in an outbuilding where Roger had left it, and we left a note in its place with our thanks. Opposite the road end of the house, a long glen ran north-westwards containing a roaring cascading river. To the west of the river, a fine wood of pines grew high and stately, and we decided to look for a camp somewhere in this vicinity. Two hundred yards from the road, we fell upon the perfect place, a narrow ledge of flat grass beside a deep rocky pool, backed and sheltered by a high grassy bank. A huge waterfall thundered into the pool, and great smooth rocks around it tempted us to a riverside brew up and feet dip. After the earlier frustrations, this was a perfect way to finish the day. We brewed tea and laced it with lemon to kill our thirsts, washed ourselves and our socks and enjoyed a magnificent supper of minestrone soup with parmesan cheese, beef curry, rice pudding and a thing called blackcurrant surprise, with coffee to finish it off. The whole meal was spiced with that indefinable flavour rendered by a hard day's walking.

A few miles down the glen, in an old dun or fortress called Dun Geal, near to where Fortingall stands today, tradition claims that an emissary of Emperor Caesar Augustus arrived on a mission of peace. As he talked with Metellanus, King of Scotland, the King's wife gave birth to a son. The son was given the name Pontius Pilate. Seton Gordon, that marvellous sennachie of Scottish lore, tells the tale of a visitor arriving at Fortingall, and asking an old man who was working on the road if he could point out the birthplace of Pontius Pilate. "I have never heard of the man," was the curt answer. "But surely," protested the visitor, "surely you go to church?" "Yes," the old man said, "but there's nobody of that name goes to my kirk."

The incessant monotony of a neighbouring cuckoo had us up at seven, and away by eight. Our spirits were high; we were well into harness now with three full days' walking behind us; the sun was shining from a clear blue sky with only a thin haze muting colours and distant sounds, and today was to be almost solely a hill day with four Munros to cross *en route* to our intended camp at Tummel Bridge.

We left our riverside paradise and struck north-eastwards up the hill opposite Beinn Dearg, a heather-covered hill with a great horseshoe plateau. We climbed up through a young forestry plantation of deep furrows to gain the summit plateau, hot and sweaty work in the hot morning sun. Eastwards, across a deep trench marked on the map as Dubh Choirein, rose our first Munro of the day, Carn Gorm, a big rounded lump, not unlike its Speyside namesake, though lacking the great size and character of the latter. We traversed around the high peaty bealach, and struck up the steep heathery slopes, Roger climbing straight up to gain the north-west ridge, and me traversing across the hillside at an angle making directly for the summit. We split up like this often on this trans-Scotland walk, enjoying our own seclusion for a while, wooing nature in solitude and silence. As I was just about to top the summit ridge, a herd of twenty deer hinds sceetered over the stony slopes no more than thirty yards in front of me, no doubt disturbed by Roger, who soon appeared close behind them. As they saw me in their path, the leading hind suddenly skidded to a stop, whilst the rest bumped into each other in a great pile-up reminiscent of the antics of the Keystone Cops.

A long ridge of short springy turf took us to Meall Garbh, another rounded lump of a hill, recorded in my log as one of the dullest hills I have climbed. Indeed all these hills are rather dull, big sprawling flat-topped puddings, their only redeeming factor being one or two well-shaped corries, still rimmed by glistening white snow cornices. Roger had recently done the round of Creag Mhor (above Glen Lyon. We missed this one out today as we had both climbed it previously and it was off our route which lay northwards rather than south), Carn Mairg, Meall Garbh, and Carn Gorm, in running shoes and shorts, completing the circuit in a few hours, enjoying the physical challenge more than the aesthetic beauty of the hills.

Due east of Meall Garbh, Carn Mairg, the Rust Coloured Cairn, the highest of the group at 3419 feet, rose from a long broad stony ridge. We left our packs at the north-eastern extremity of the summit ridge, and boulder hopped, feeling as light and free as a bird, to the summit. From here, the long high ridge of Schiehallion dominated all to the north. All morning it had appeared dim through the veil of haze, but now it rose unhesitatingly, rocky and steep, from the dark depths of Gleann Mor. We had a decision to make: whether to drop down into Gleann Mor and climb the steep south slopes of the hill, or to try and keep as much height as possible and make our way by a series of high linking ridges to the high bealach which separates the western slopes of Schiehallion from Geal Charn. We went for the second option.

On reflection it was a good choice, though at the time, as we wallowed in vast acreages of peatbog, we doubted it. Just below Geal Charn, we came upon a narrow track, which led us up to a stone bothy tucked away into the rocky south-east slopes of the hill. It could have been a superb hut, built from local stone with a tin roof, but unfortunately the building itself, and the surrounding slopes, were a mass of litter; wine bottles, beer cans, polythene bags, bags of hardened cement; it was a sickening scene. Even worse was the crudely gouged road which ran up to it from Kinloch Rannoch. This had been carelessly blasted and bulldozed from the hillside, the soil deposits and rubble fringing a great white weal which could be seen for miles; a work of grotesque vandalism, especially in a designated Area of Outstanding Natural Beauty as this is.

Fuming, internally because of the desecration of a hillside for the dubious benefit of a privileged few who refuse to walk to shoot their sport, and externally by the very hot sun which was now trying its damndest to frazzle us, we dropped down to the heathery bealach below Schiehallion and took a break.

Schiehallion is the Fairy Hill of the Caledonians, but it could be described as the Fairy Hill which Weighed the Earth. The almost perfect cone shape of the hill, when viewed from the west, prompted the Astronomer Royal, Neville Maskelyne, in 1774, to conduct experiments on it to try and determine the earth's weight and mass. One of the side issues to come out of the experiments was the linking of similar heights on a map by lines. Charles Hutton, a Fellow of the Royal Society of Astronomers, was responsible for undertaking most of the calculations on the experiments, and in his examination of the survey data, hit upon the first recorded use of contour lines, map lines which we now take so much for granted in representing mountain shapes.

Schiehallion is a big hill, a totally isolated mountain of quartzite, which has weathered evenly to produce its distinctive cone shape. Neil Munro, the Argyllshire novelist, once described it, when viewed from Rannoch Moor in the west, thus: "The end of it [Rannoch Moor] was lost in mist from which jutted, like a skerry of the sea, Schiehallion."

Contouring around to the north, we started climbing the quartzite slopes from the north-west ridge, and soon came across the tourist track which comes up from Tempar, on the Kinloch Rannoch road. We climbed slowly, each step wringing the perspiration from our brow, dripping into the eyes and nipping. On and on went the loose crumbly scree of the track, then over some large square-cut boulders of quartzite, and on to the summit. The view, if you are lucky, is an extensive one, from the wide open approaches, to the mountain jumbles of the west, and into the very heart of the Grampians in the east. Today everything was ludicrously diffused by the confounded haze, and we could barely distinguish our hills of the morning.

We descended eastwards to the Braes of Foss, down the long peaty track, which today, being dry, was a pure delight. We ran much of the way, bouncing down on the springy peat with none of the usual knee jarring of normal running descents. A spring of cold, clear water gave us a brief respite, and on we went, through a gate into a field of sheep, and then over another gate on to the roadside.

The long heather-clad ridge of Craig Kynachan separated us from our night's camp at Tummel Bridge, where a commercial campsite with showers, a restaurant, and a bar would allow us to wash some clothes, ourselves, and drown the inner man, who was rapidly beginning to feel like a parched strip of sandpaper.

Curlews warbled as we climbed steadily through the heather; a herd of deer scattered to the four corners as we approached, and grouse went clattering away from under our feet, their guttural coarseness like bronchial old men arguing in a pub. Long coarse heather, in some places thigh deep, slowed us down on our descent, scratching, tugging and tearing at our bare legs. Roger, for the first time on the walk, showed impatience, cursing loudly at the clagging undergrowth. The heather was too deep to allow us to see what was underneath, and subsequently, we stumbled over boulders, fell into streams, and sloshed through peaty bog. It was hard going, but the monotony was alleviated considerably near to Tummel Bridge, when we came across a very young deer fawn. Big-eyed and inquisitive, stilting along on spindly legs, it was obviously very young, and it showed no fear of us at all. It was tempting to touch it, fondle it, for it was an appealing little creature, but no doubt its mother was lying close by watching us intently. We moved on, and left it as it was.

Tummel Bridge Camping and Caravan Site was a godsend today. We were soon enjoying the steamy comforts of hot showers, painful initially on sun-scorched skin. My culinary aspirations were given a great boost when Roger suggested we just cook another meal in the tent, rather than sample the restaurant fare, but we did sample the campsite bar before turning in for an early night, burnt, sore and happy. (For those who shun such luxuries and desire to camp wild, there are one or two good pitches high on the shoulder of Craig Kynachan. Permission at Braes of Foss.)

Leave Tummel Bridge eastwards on the B8019, and go for just over 4 miles to point GR 832599. Go through the gate beside the road and follow the faint path which becomes more obvious as the hill is climbed northwards. Follow the path N. and N.E., climb the Forestry Commission stile and pass the north shore of Lochan nan Nighean. Path is very indistinct hereabouts due to young plantations. Cross wall into mature plantation and follow the bulldozed forestry road to farm at Edintian, $2\frac{1}{4}$ miles. Go through farmyard, turn first left, and follow old path N. then N.E. over fields and past Tomanraid, and then N. down steep slopes through birch woods to cross bridge over R. Garry to Blair Atholl, $2\frac{1}{4}$ miles. Leave Blair Atholl northwards by the Fenderbridge road, bearing right at Fenderbridge to follow the road uphill to Loch Moraig, $2\frac{1}{2}$ miles. Continue on bulldozed track for 1 mile, then cut across heather moors to slopes of Carn Liath. Camp.

Next day was, in effect, a rest day. No mountains to climb, no long sections of road, only a hop over to Blair Atholl, to collect a food parcel from the railway station, and a leisurely wander up towards Carn Liath, the first of the Beinn a'Ghlo group.

We left the campsite after a mad shopping spree, (we bought much more than we needed but couldn't resist the temptation) and followed the road, the B8019, eastwards on the north shore of Loch Tummel for about $4\frac{1}{4}$ miles, to where an old track left the road northwards, and climbed up in a series of zigzags over the rich pastures towards Lochan nan Nighean. On this stretch of road we walked for about a mile with no map, the top right-hand corner of Sheet 51 and the bottom left-hand corner of Sheet 43 just missing the short section of road. To get that section on map, we would have to have carried another map, Sheet 52, but that would only have been excessive weight. We happily went without it, hardly being able to lose ourselves on a mile stretch of road.

We stopped for a while by Lochan nan Nighean, a place loud with the cacophony of black-headed gulls. A roebuck observed us from across the loch before bounding off into the forest, and a moorcock crawed from somewhere in the trees. The track we took is a good short cut, a 5-mile jaunt over fields, forest and high moorland, rather than the 12-mile alternative slog around the roads. It was hot again, and already the great ridge of Schiehallion behind us was lost in a haze. Loch Tummel shimmered in the heat, a loch of great beauty with its well-manicured banks and rounded hills on either side, rising to the giants of the Beinn a'Ghlo group beyond its head in the east.

According to the map, our track runs through the forest to where it meets a forestry road, leading after a short while out of the trees to a farm called Edintian. We lost the path, typically, in a young forest plantation which seemed to have been planted completely over where the path should have been. By taking some compass bearings, we eventually burst from the trees, and found we had missed the main forestry road by only a few hundred yards. More importantly, we could see the farm, Edintian, down below us.

The track from here is delightful, passing through the farmyard where we were greeted by a loud farm dog, contouring up easy slopes, and past a rather picturesque cottage, complete with a garden of rhododendron bushes. To the north, below us, the white ramparts of Blair Atholl Castle shone in the sun, and beyond it, the high rounded hills of the southern Cairngorms and the tree-clad valley of the Tilt. Steep slopes led us through birch woods down to the River Garry, and the bridge over into the old village of Blair Atholl.

A rejuvenated and restored water mill turned out to be a tea-room, and we took half an hour of indolent bliss, drinking tea from dainty cups and enjoying freshly made scones and jam. We bought some wholemeal rolls for lunch, and wandered down to the railway station, where I collected my food parcel. I had packed away one or two goodies, including a can of fruit salad. Rather than carry it too far, we walked through the village, stopping at the store for some soft drinks, and wandered up by the Old Bridge of Tilt, where we found an idyllic lunch spot, beside a small burn in the cool shade of some large oaks. As was appropriate on this, a rest day, we lingered over lunch; fresh wheaten rolls with soft cheese and *pâte*, followed by the fruit salad laced with lager and lime from a can. All was enjoyed on the bank of the burn, with feet dangling in the cold clear water. Idyllic.

The rest of the day was passed in a sun-scorched memory of easy ambling up the road by Loch Moraig, another haunt of noisy seagulls, and following the track which runs north-eastwards, just skirting the southern slopes of cone-shaped Carn Liath. With the prospect of another sunset, we climbed steadily, if slowly, up the bracken-covered slopes to around the 2000-foot contour, where a flattish shelf in the heather and bracken allowed us to pitch the tent.

We put on a brew, washed some clothes in the burn, and lay back for a relaxed evening. Ten minutes later Roger got up, wandered around the tent, looking uncomfortable. I felt restless too, and the attraction of lazing around all evening suddenly didn't look so appealing. Our easy day had left us with a surfeit of energy. Looking up towards the summit of Carn Liath, only a thousand feet or so above us, Roger half suggested that it might be a nice idea to wander up for the view. He didn't have to ask twice; within minutes we were on our way, almost running up the steep rocky upper slopes, using up an abundance of energy which had been irritating us. As we climbed, the haze which had been lingering all day quickly merged into high cloud, ruling out the possibilities of a sunset, and spoiling the view from the summit. Braigh Coire Chruinn Bhalgain and Beinn a'Ghlo itself were just a dark mass in the north, our hills for tomorrow before heading north-eastwards to Loch nan Eun, high in the Cairnwell Hills of the southern Cairngorms.

Leave slopes of Carn Liath and traverse due E. for $1\frac{1}{2}$ miles, until you come across the footpath which runs N.N.E. from Shinagag. Follow the path, which after a while becomes a bulldozed track, past the mouth of Glen Loch and then S.E. to Daldhu, $5\frac{1}{2}$ miles. Walk N. on track beside the Allt Fearnach for 4 miles, and then strike due E. into Gleann Mor. Follow the glen to the high bealach between Carn an Righ and Mam nan Carn, $2\frac{1}{4}$ miles. Ascend Carn an Righ, 3377 feet, retrace steps back down to the bealach, and follow path over peaty ground for $1\frac{1}{4}$ miles to Loch nan Eun. Camp. Leave the loch and follow high ridges eastwards over Carn a'Chlarsaich, Creag Easgaidh, N. top of Carn Bhinnein, Carn a'Gheoidh, 3194 feet, Carn nan Sac, and then N.N.E. for $\frac{3}{4}$ mile before swinging due E. to descend the slopes between Carn Aosda and the Cairnwell, 5 miles. Descend through ski-ground slopes, cross the A93 road, and climb through more ski paraphernalia to Meall Odhar and Glas Maol. Camp on slopes of Glas Maol.

As it happened, it was just as well we climbed Carn Liath that night. Next morning dawned in a flurry of drizzle and low cloud. A plover mourned on and on, a sad sound in that dripping environment. We knew that our proposed walk over the Beinn a'Ghlo Hills and then on to Loch nan Eun was a stiff test, hard enough in good conditions, but in these wet and cloudy conditions it would have been a bit miserable. We abandoned our plans, and decided on a low-level course.

Contouring the rocky and heather-clad slopes of Carn Liath eastwards, we eventually dropped down and found the footpath which runs north east by the Allt Coire Lagain, a wet and boggy path which was frustratingly indistinct in places. After our high spirits of the previous two days it was back to earth with a thump, and a squelch! Our path poured on, turned into a landrover track, and passed the entrance to Glen Loch, before turning south-eastwards towards Gleann Fearnach. A tiny bothy by the Allt Glen Loch gave us some shelter for a break, a remote little building probably used only by shooting parties and the odd stravaiging gangrel. Two miles down the track, 2 miles in which I counted more hares than I have ever seen in my life before, some of them as large as dogs, we turned north again at Daldhu, and followed the track by the Allt Fearnach for 4 miles, before dropping down eastwards into Gleann Mor, a long glen which runs below the steep slopes of Carn an Righ.

Occasionally one holds memories of places which are special for some reason. Perhaps the scenery is particularly grand, perhaps you just felt on top of the world at that particular spot, but Gleann Mor sketched itself indelibly in my mind for its superb atmosphere of loneliness and wild bare beauty. Long and curving, it lies between the steep slopes of Carn an Righ in the north and the long ridge of Glas Tulaichean in the south. Trout were jumping in the river, a family of dippers darted upstream, and the green mossy riverbanks were now gleaming in the sun, the drizzle of the morning at last thrown off.

We followed the curve of the glen, and climbed on to the high bealach which separates Carn an Righ, the King's Cairn, from Mam nan Carn. Loch nan Eun, our destination for the night, was only a mile away to the east, at the very head of Gleann Mor, and as it was only 4 p.m., we could afford to take our time and enjoy a packless ascent of Carn an Righ. Three Munros surround the high bowl of Loch nan Eun, the loch of birds, and we wanted to climb them before we left for the Cairnwell in the morning. Taking our time, we were up and back down Carn an Righ within half an hour, the walking easy on good crisp heather and alpine mossy grasslands. Collecting the packs, we wandered leisurely round to Loch nan Eun through a desert of peat hags, the path sketchy in places, soaking up the real wilderness atmosphere of the place, the home of ptarmigan, dunlin, dotterel and mountain hares, typical residents of the arctic-alpine zone.

The loch itself is a blue jewel set in a high bowl amongst 3000-foot tops, its lapping waters 2550 feet above the level of the sea. We camped on the south side of the loch, beside the ruins of some ancient shieling. A quick brew slaked the thirst, and we were off again, north-westwards towards Mam nan Carn, and over the connecting ridge to Beinn Iutharn Mor, our second Munro of the day. Beinn Iutharn Mor, 3424 feet, the Big Hill of Hell, is indeed a big hill, with its great bulging shoulders thrusting in all directions dominating the surrounding hills. For the first time since Cruachan, the views were extensive, over the greens, browns and ochres of this vast rolling tableland, and on northwards towards the snow-capped Cairngorms. I spent a few minutes reciting their names to Roger, from the hills of the Moine Mhor across to Beinn Avon, feeling a pang of nostalgia for these, my hills of home. Many people have cast a slur on these high hills of the southern Cairngorms, and they may be more featureless than the peaks and pinnacles of the west, but they have an atmospheric quality which is unique. They are big hills, remote, with vast wide-open views and great wide skies; up here you know you are on the roof of Scotland.

Next morning I wasn't so sure. A peasouper of a mist had rolled in overnight, and the continuous drizzle of yesterday morning had turned to genuine rain. A quick breakfast, and we trotted up Glas Tulaichean, 3449 feet, behind us, a straightforward ridge ascent even with only twenty yards of visibility, our noses following compass needles to locate the tent again on our return. As usual, our spirits had dropped with the barometer, and it was a great temptation to get back into the sleeping-bags again for a couple of hours instead of packing up the tent and moving off towards the Cairnwell. We tempted each other with the thought of hot pies and chips at the

Cairnwell ski ground café, and with this thought dangling in front of us like a carrot, we squelched off through the murk to follow the curving line of ridges towards Cairnwell. On a clear day this ridge is obvious, from Loch nan Eun to Carn a'Chlarsaich, the northern top of Carn Bhinnein, Carn a'Gheoidh, the only Munro on the ridge, Carn nan Sac, and the high bealach between Carn Aosda and the Cairnwell itself. On a day like ours with driving rain and thick mist, it wasn't quite so simple, and I simply lagged back and let Roger get on with it. Nose to compass, he valiantly led us eastwards, making only one little mistake which dropped us a few hundred feet below our course before we realized that we were in the wrong place.

By the time we reached the Cairnwell we were soaked through, cold, and very hungry, our low spirits really crashing at the sight of the erosion and rubbish which decorates the summer ski grounds of Cairnwell. This area shares a distinction with Coire Cas of Cairngorm, near Aviemore, in being one of Scotland's major ski areas, but whilst the management at Coire Cas go to great lengths to prevent erosion and, indeed, spend a lot of money on reseeding projects, the slopes of Cairnwell show a distinct lack of care with the haphazard development. To make matters worse, all we could get to eat in the café was a cheese roll and a chocolate biscuit. Hot pies, chips and delicacies, we were told, are sold only during the ski season! As we left, grumbling and still hungry, we felt sorry for the coachload of old age pensioners who had just arrived. With the rain and cold, low mist and depressing scenery of the ski paraphernalia, it must have seemed like the end of the world rather than the "Bonnie Scotland" which their bus proclaimed from its front window.

It was almost four o'clock, and anxious as we were to leave the scarred and gouged hillsides, we couldn't, as the wind on the Glas Maol plateau which lay ahead of us was too strong to pitch a tent. We had no alternative but to pitch amidst the swaying pylon lines, beer-can infested streams, and oil-stained slopes. I would suggest that anyone following this route should camp somewhere west of Cairnwell, possibly in the Loch Vrotachan area, or time their journey so that they can wander down beyond the old Devil's Elbow road, south of the Cairnwell, and camp there.

From Glas Maol, 3504 feet, walk N. over broad ridge for $1\frac{1}{2}$ miles before swinging N.E. for $1\frac{1}{2}$ miles to Cairn of Claise, 3484 feet. Walk due N. for $\frac{3}{4}$ mile then swing N.W. to Carn an Tuirc, 3340 feet. Return to Cairn of Claise. Walk due E. for $1\frac{1}{2}$ miles to Tom Buidhe, 3140 feet, then N.N.W. for $\frac{1}{2}$ mile to Tolmount, 3143 feet. Head N., passing edge of Glen Callater, for $1\frac{1}{4}$ miles to Fafernie, then $\frac{1}{2}$ mile E.N.E. to Cairn Bannoch, 3314 feet, then 1 mile S.E. to Broad Cairn, 3268 feet. Continue over Broad Cairn in a S.W. direction to the small bothy above Corrie Chash, 1 mile, and then drop down due S. by zigzag footpath to Bachnagairn, $\frac{3}{4}$ mile. Follow bulldozed track from Bachnagairn to campsite at Acharn, $3\frac{1}{2}$ miles. Glendoll Youth Hostel is just $\frac{1}{2}$ mile west of Acharn. Camp or use Youth Hostel.

Follow the minor road S.E. to Clova, 4 miles, then the B955 for 10 miles to Cortachy. Follow minor roads for 2 miles to Memus, 4 miles to Tannadice, then the B057 to the A94 at Finavon, $1\frac{1}{2}$ miles. Follow the A94 for 7 miles to Brechin, then, finally, the last 8 miles on the A945 to Montrose.

During the night, the wind began to gust stronger, and by morning the rains had been blown away. The sky was clear, with only the odd fluffy cloud scudding across the horizon in the breeze. Half an hour took us to the summit of Glas Maol, 3504 feet, a big rounded top sitting on the edge of the Caenlochan National Nature Reserve. It seemed incredible that such litter and erosion had been allowed to occur so close to a Nature Reserve, and indeed, we passed two old car tyres at an altitude of 3000 feet, only a few hundred yards from the Nature Conservancy sign. Clearly a management plan of some sort should be established for these hills before it becomes too late, as it may be already.

Today was our last day on the tops before the last hard

batter on the roads to Montrose. To end with a bang, we planned seven Munros, before dropping down into Glen Clova and a night of comparative luxury in the Youth Hostel at Glendoll.

From the Glas Maol, a path runs across the broad ridge north-eastwards to Cairn of Claise, where we left our packs by the stone wall which crosses the hill. Forty-five minutes of easy walking over springy sedge and alpine grasses took us out to Carn an Tuirc, the Hill of the Boar, 3340 feet, and back again for ten minutes of chocolate munching in the lee of the stone wall. Almost 2 miles to the east, the wee dumpy Munro of Tom Buidhe rises from the great tableland of greens and browns, a great plateau stretching 6 or 7 miles north to the great bulk of Lochnagar, and eastwards, for 6 miles, towards the Braes o'Angus. Lacking the sheer desolation of the high Cairngorms, these southern Grampians are far more fertile, thanks mainly to their lime-rich rocks and deeper richer soils. In fact, the lime-rich soil of Caenlochan, just east of Glas Maol, ranks with Ben Lawers in Perthshire as one of the prime sites in Britain of uncommon arctic-alpine plants.

The two-mile stretch of wilderness to Tom Buidhe, and then across to Tolmount, is a deer-infested place, alive with the cackling of ptarmigan and the joyful outpourings of skylarks. Dotterel and dunlin nest in these high wastes, and you may be lucky in seeing eagle or peregrine who nest in the few remote crags which fringe the corries. Tolmount's great redeeming feature (as a Munro summit it is barely a rise in the ground) is the views it offers down Glen Callater, its upper reaches a wild and impressive place, hemmed in by crags and steep broken rocks.

A cairned footpath runs over the high watershed north-east of Tolmount, an old right of way called Jocks Road. According to an old Cairngorm Club Journal the path is named after one John Winters. This is a popular through route from Glendoll to Braemar, via Loch Callater, and for those not wanting to snatch the remaining two or three Munros on this walk, provides a

quick and easy descent to Glendoll. The hills north of us —
Fafernie (not a Munro), Carn an t-Sagairt Mor, Cairn Bannoch
and Broad Cairn — were all new to Roger, and so we split up on
the summit of Fafernie, he off to bag Sagairt Mor, one mile
N.N.W. of Fafernie, and I to wander leisurely over the rocky
crests of Cairn Bannoch and Broad Cairn, hoping to snatch
some photographs of the rocky depths which hold the Dubh
Loch, immediately north of Broad Cairn. Over the crisp
herbiage of the plateau I went, past the cairn of Cairn Bannoch,
and on towards Broad Cairn, a stony conical hill with more
appeal than most of its near neighbours. I wandered down the
northern slopes of the hill, and managed to get my photographs
of crag-fast Dubh Loch, a deep-set ribbon of water not unlike
Loch Avon in the Cairngorms, although a lot smaller. Back over
Broad Cairn, a peaty footpath leads to a land rover track below
the eastern shoulder of the hill. The views eastwards down the
length of Loch Muick were impressive, with great broiling
clouds filling the horizon. This is Balmoral country, so if you see
a couple of corgis prancing over the hill in front of you, practise
your curtsy!

A mile E.S.E. of the summit of Cairn Bannoch, a narrow path
runs due south from the land rover track, from beside a semi-
derelict hut, down towards the tumbling waters of the Esk, and
the larches and pines of Bachnagairn in upper Glen Clova. I
waited for about forty minutes to allow Roger to catch me up,
before heading down this path, zigzagging our way down from
the last hill of the trip.

As we wandered down the glen, Roger remarked that this
was, in effect, the end of the walk as far as he was concerned. I
agreed, the remaining thirty-odd miles of road bashing was
only to be justified as part of the Trans-Scotland concept, the
coast-to-coast enterprise, which really was relatively
unimportant to us.

Danny Smith, the hill-walking warden of Glendoll Youth
Hostel, welcomed us, and we blethered until late into the night,
after consuming a large meal of stew, potatoes, rice pudding

and fruit. It was a bit strange sleeping in a proper bed, and we both missed the scents of a westerly breeze floating through the open door of a tent.

Next morning dawned wet, which probably was a good thing as it would keep us cool for the long walk on the roads. The road out of Glen Clova is long and straight, 4 miles to the inn at Clova, then around the bend onto the B955 for the long climb out of the glen. We kept with the B955 for 10 miles to Cortachy, past the grounds of its castle and on to minor roads which carried us along great straight stretches through Memus, to Tannadice, a pleasant village of high hedgerows and quaint little houses. A mile and a half on the B957 brought us on to the busy A94, and started us off on 7 miles of traffic dodging to Brechin, a linen- and paper-making Royal Burgh. We considered stopping here for the night, one or two comfortable bed and breakfast establishments looked snug and comfortable in the wet and dull evening light, but with the bit grimly between our teeth, we decided we might as well just bash on, especially since Montrose was only 8 miles away. A phone call to a hotel in Montrose booked a bed for us, and off we went into the rain again, 8 weary miles of drudgery, the spray from passing cars soaking us to the skin. Soon, the church steeple of Montrose came into sight, and two and a half hours after leaving Brechin we arrived in Montrose, deciding that the customary boot in the sea could wait until morning. Bed that night was seventh heaven, and we didn't really care, or notice, the lack of a westerly breeze through the tent door.

ROUTE 2: RATHAD NAM MEIRLEACH: THE THIEVES' ROAD

About 80 miles. A four-camp low-level backpacking route following in the footsteps of the western clans who used the Thieves' Road from Lochaber through Badenoch to Moray.

Maps required: O.S. 1:50,000 Second Series. Sheets 36, 35, 42, 41, 43.

From Ryvoan Bothy, follow track S.W. for $2\frac{1}{2}$ miles to Glenmore. Follow ski road S. for $\frac{1}{2}$ mile to point marked on map as "toll". Turn due W., enter forest, and follow trail along S. shore of Loch Morlich for $1\frac{3}{4}$ miles until you reach boundary fence. Cross fence by stile, and continue N.W. for $\frac{1}{4}$ mile before turning S. on Rothiemurchus Lodge track. Follow this track S.S.W. for almost 1 mile before crossing stile into forest on your right. Follow trail to Cairngorm Club footbridge, 2 miles, and shortly afterwards (150 yards) turn due W. for Loch an Eilein. Cairngorm Club footbridge to Loch an Eilein is $1\frac{3}{4}$ miles. Follow the trail on S. shore of Loch an Eilein and S. shore of Loch Gamhna and continue S.W. Ford the narrow Allt Coire Follais, and follow path past Inshriach Bothy to Forestry Commission fence, $2\frac{1}{4}$ miles. Follow path on S. side of fence for 200 yards, before turning S. over river flats. Cross river and climb stile into forest. Walk S.W. through forest to Glen Feshie, 2 miles. Follow public road S. in Glen Feshie for 4 miles to Achlean. Follow path beside R. Feshie S. to Ruigh Aiteachain, $3\frac{1}{2}$ miles. Bothy or camp.

It was six o'clock in the evening when I arrived at the bothy at Ryvoan, on the edge of the Glenmore Forest Park some 8 or 9 miles east of Aviemore. Earlier in the afternoon I had camped in the Forestry Commission campsite at Glenmore, a magnificent camping ground surrounded by pine forests and overlooked by the great bulk of the northern corries of Cairngorm, and after an early dinner I strolled the 3 miles through the picturesque Ryvoan Pass, which runs past the National Mountaineering Centre at Glenmore Lodge.

This, in effect, was both the beginnings and the end of a very old trail, the end of a stealthy march by Lochaber clansmen in days long ago, a furtive journey through the quiet backwaters of the old district of Badenoch, a journey which took them through here, the Pass of Ryvoan, towards the rich pastures, and rich takings, of Morayshire. Ryvoan was also the start of the return trip home, a more hazardous journey, the thieves driving the herds of stolen cattle back along the same route, in the greatest of haste, anxious to put as many miles between them and the plundered lands of Moray, before daylight.

This was a time when many of the western clans believed they had a divine right to lift the booty of the fertile Laich of Moray, an attitude summed up in a letter sent by Allan Cameron of Lochiel in 1645 to the Laird of Grant. In the letter, Lochiel apologizes most profusely for injuries inflicted on one of the Grants by some Cameron freebooters, explaining that the reivers had not known the poor victim was a Grant, but thought that he was a Morayman. Later in the letter, it was recorded that the raid was intended to be "to Morrayland, quhair all men taks their prey".

This ancient route was known as Rathad nam Meirleach, or the Caterans' Road (Thieves' or Robbers' Road), and not only was it the most direct route from Lochaber through Badenoch to Morayshire, but it avoided the populous croftships and villages of Speyside, where the Lochaber men would no doubt have been severely resisted.

I sat for a while against the gable end of the old bothy at Ryvoan, and gazed across the ancient Abernethy forests to the fertile hills of Moray. From the pass, the reivers would have crossed the Braes of Abernethy, probably at night, and rounded up the cattle of Dorback, Tomintoul and the surrounding districts, arriving back at Ryvoan with their grunting, sweating

Campsite on Cruachan

Sunset from Cruachan

Roger Smith in Glen Kinglass

Approaching Loch Dochard

Treats at Blair Atholl railway station

Roger Smith on Glas Maol

The great sweep of Beinn Iutharn Mor in the southern Cairngorms

The vast open landscape of the Grampians

Backpackers in Glen
Feshie

Loch an Eilein Castle

Evening camp on Rathad nam Meirleach

Achlean in Glen Feshie

Culra Lodge Bothy

The wire bridge at Steall in upper Glen Nevis

booty. A bulldozed track nowadays runs up from Nethybridge, the final miles of a recently opened Speyside Way, a 70-mile long-distance footpath from Spey Bay on the Moray coast, following the River Spey, before leaving its banks to meander up through the old forests of Abernethy to come by way of Ryvoan to finish at Glenmore.

From the bare purple moors of Abernethy and Ryvoan, the track through the Pass between Creag Loisgte and Creag nan Gall, appropriately the Hill of the Stranger, comes in rich contrast. Below the scree-girt heights, pines, larches, birches and juniper grow in luxuriant profusion on a valley floor lush in green bracken, bilberry, cowberry and heather. Even much of the track itself does not yield to the tread of man, carpeting itself in mosses, mixed with the natural litter of pine needles, cones, fallen twigs and branches. In the still summer evening, not even the voracity of the midges could spoil the magical qualities of this pass, a place, not surprisingly, long associated with the Little People. Here, at moonglow, the fairies are said to come quietly and wash their emerald green clothing in the waters of An Lochan Uaine, a deep pool of aquamarine translucence surrounded by rocks and twisted and gnarled Scots pines.

The patch continues in its natural beauty for another few hundred yards, until a high deer fence abruptly divides what is natural growth from the infinitely less appealing man-made plantations, their uniformity and close planting producing a dark suffocating mass of pine foliage. It was hereabouts that Robin Oig, a Glenmore hunter, once came upon a green-clad fairy playing a tiny set of bagpipes. Robin snatched the pipes, and threw down his bonnet in exchange, only to see it vanish into thin air, leaving in his hand a dead puffball to which three blades of grass were attached.

Back at the campsite in Glenmore, all peaceful thoughts of fairies were banished from my thoughts in the vast conglomeration of people who were now filling up every nook and cranny in the site. It was back to reality with a thud. Sleep didn't come easy that night, and I dozed on and off to a background of banging car doors, transistor radios and screaming bairns, the cacophony of a mid-summer commercial campsite in the Scottish Highlands.

Morning couldn't come quick enough, and I was up and away by eight o'clock, southwards on the ski road for a quarter of a mile, and then into the forest on a track which runs adjacent to the southern shore of Loch Morlich. It was a misty morning, with the promise of a good day ahead and, although cool, it was fresh and pleasant in the forest, far away from the now slumbering campsite. This track by Loch Morlich is thought to be the original route of the Caterans' Road, and leads after a while into the great Forest of Rothiemurchus, ancient home of the Clans Shaw and Grant.

The forest track wound on, now and then rising high above the gently lapping waters of the loch, the morning mists now shimmering gently and slowly lifting as though the whole loch was exhaling in the early morning air. Loch Morlich is a geological "kettle hole", simply a great hole surrounded by glacial drift, and its outlet, the Allt Luineag, carving a slot westwards through the glacial debris and moraines. This geological description is an unfeeling one, for Loch Morlich is a fine stretch of water, fringed by golden beaches and backed by a solid wall of 4000-foot mountain, whose long-lying snow slopes, in winter and spring, contrast vividly with the dark green forest of the foothills between loch and mountain.

Several roe deer bounded across the track in front of me, ethereal in the still evaporating mists, their coats a bright brownish red. As I walked quietly around one particular bend in the track, I came upon a young doe, browsing at the edge of the forest above the road. I stopped and froze, and slowly reached for my camera which was hanging from my rucksack strap. Never have I seen such an attractive beast; her movements all had a winning abruptness, from the jaunty way she picked up her legs as she moved from patch to patch, to the jerky flicking of her tail. Just as I managed to focus on her, she suddenly looked at me, warned by some ancient animal instinct, and in that brief moment that her dark liquid eyes met mine through the lens of the camera, I was so totally and utterly bewitched by her guileless innocence that I could not press the shutter release. Her nose was black and twitching slightly and around it the short wax-smooth pelage was white, contrasting richly with the dark redness of the rest of her. But it was her eyes which enchanted me, so dark, so impenetrable, showing no sign of the fear which her instincts so surely must have been signalling to her. As quickly as she looked up at me she was gone, vanished in a blur of total precision and perfect deportment so fast, that I barely had time to take the picture. As it happened, all I managed to get on record was a blurred image of a flashing warning tail as she turned to bound into the trees, but I was left with a much more important experience than a mere photographic snapshot: an almost overwhelming wonder of the immensity of that moment as I gazed eye to eye into the beautiful world of nature. If I had been carrying a gun rather than a camera, I would have broken it over my knee and thrown the pieces away in that blinding moment, rather than attempt to take the life of something so innocent and exquisite.

For the rest of that day I felt as high as though I had been floating on a cloud, and the magnificent surroundings that I walked through only served to exaggerate the bond which I believed had been formed between me and this natural vibrant world. I crossed a stile into the Rothiemurchus Estate and, after a short distance, took a rough bulldozed road southwards for half a mile before turning south-westwards back into the forest again.

The track now meandered through a natural lavishness of Scots pine, birch and juniper, growing from a thick undergrowth ungrazed by either sheep or deer, a landscape altered very little since the days when much of Scotland lay under the great mattress which was the ancient Caledonian pine forest. Blaeberries abounded here, ripe and luscious in

July, and I passed carpets rich in cowberry, or cranberry, their white bell-like flowers and shiny evergreen leaves only just losing their bloom.

On I went, past the signpost which indicates the track which straggles up through the increasingly stunted pines until it emerges high above the great forest on the glacial moraines at the entrance to the Lairig Ghru, the old right of way through the Cairngorms from Speyside to Deeside. There was no Lairig Ghru for me today though, but I had no misgivings on passing the trail as I dropped down towards the confluence of the Allt Druidh and the Am Beanaidh, the latter river used centuries ago for floating timber down from Glen Einich to the River Spey at Inverdruie, where it was floated downriver to the coast.

I stopped by the Iron Bridge which crosses the river here, erected by the Aberdeen-based Cairngorm Club and named as such on the Ordnance Survey map. As I chewed some sandwiches, chaffinches, tits and pied wagtails flirted around me, eager to catch a crumb, the tiny tits showing a brave aggression towards the larger birds.

The morning mists had long since dissipated, and the sun now shone hot from a clear sky. The scent of pine resin drifted heavy in the air, and it was refreshing to leave the forest behind for the cooler open moorland which stretches westwards to the forest which surrounds Loch an Eilein. This moorland was once forested too, but constant fellings during the two wars have left it as it is today. To the south, great heather-clad slopes lead steeply to Creag Dubh, the beginning of the 5-mile-long Sguran ridge. It was this long ridge that I spent the rest of the day going round, by the southern shore of Loch an Eilein and into the forests of Inshriach, before entering the majestic confines of Glen Feshie.

Like the south shore of Loch Morlich, the track which twists round the southern shore of Loch an Eilein is also part of the original Caterans' Road. Today it is managed, in conjunction with Rothiemurchus Estate, by the Nature Conservancy Council, who have turned the old reivers' way into a Nature

Trail. To my mind, and in the opinion of many others, Loch an Eilein is one of the most scenic lochs in the Highlands. Completely surrounded by natural pine woods, it is an ornithologist's paradise, and even in the brief hour or so that I walked along its southern shore I saw siskin, wrens, chaffinch, crested tits, blue and coal tits, wagtails, and across the loch, spiralling high above the summit of Ord Ban, a buzzard. Admittedly I spend a lot of time in these woods living as I do only a few miles away, and on this trip I knew exactly where to look for the various species, but you can be just as lucky, and may even be luckier and spot golden eagle, capercaillie, heron, treecreepers, crossbills, or maybe even an osprey fishing for trout in the loch. The loch itself supports an abundance of wildlife, and contains brown trout, eels and pike, and otters.

Across the waters, near the northern shore of the loch, lies the island which gives this loch its name, proudly bearing the last remains of its castle. Dating from the days of Robert the Bruce, Loch an Eilein Castle has been used by Comyns, Shaws and Grants, and legend has it that the infamous Wolf of Badenoch, one Alexander Stewart, the bastard son of Robert II of Scotland once had a lair on the island stronghold.

In more recent times, the rare osprey used to build its nest there, but systematic robbing of the eggs year after year discouraged the adult birds and virtually wiped out the osprey in the Scottish Highlands. They have returned, of course, one of the happiest ornithological events of the twentieth century, but even today, the greed of man still hangs as a serious threat over the future of these magnificent fish hawks.

The Nature Trail around Loch an Eilein is a busy and popular one, and I passed quite a number of happy ramblers enjoying the scenery and the warm summer afternoon. At the south-western corner of the loch, a smaller stretch of water tags on almost as an afterthought; Loch Gamhna, a typical shallow reedy loch of the glaciated plain type. Backed by the rocky crags and pines of Kennapole Hill, known locally as the Cats Den, Loch Gamhna has a tranquillity which Loch an Eilein and Loch

Morlich both lack, grand as they may be. There are usually fewer folk here too, despite the fact that there is a good track running around the edge of the loch. As I walked along the path I flushed a goosander, and glimpsed the occasional mallard and teal as they hid themselves away in the abundant reeds which fringe the water of the loch.

As the path straggles away from the shore, I crossed a long stretch of heather-covered moorland, forded the shallow waters of the Allt Coire Follais which flows down between the pine-covered slopes of Creag Follais and Creag Fhiaclach, the highest natural tree-line you will find anywhere in Britain, and then entered the stillness of yet another ancient forest. I soon came across a clearing which houses the small wooden cabin of Inshriach Bothy, a beautiful glade amongst the ancient pines, birches and dense juniper. Lorded over by a magnificent rowan tree, it was the perfect place for a mid-afternoon snack, the coolness sweet with the heady fragrance of bog myrtle and pine. As I ate, dragonflies whirred around me and chaffinches darted from branch to branch above. It was a sore temptation to stop here for the night, pitching my tent on the luxurious grass which carpeted the clearing, but I had an equally enchanting place in mind for the night's camp, Glen Feshie, a deer-haunted glen which is one of my favourite places in the Highlands.

On I went over the winding track, past the dried-up silt and reeds of Lochan Gorm to the very edge of the Forestry plantation of Inshriach. Here, a crude gouged-out track runs westwards parallel to the Forestry fence, and I took it, rather than cross into the dense forest. After a few hundred yards, another track leaves the boulders and rubble, crosses a small stream by way of a bridge, and then crosses a wide flood plain to the south. On the western bank of the stream, a stile crosses a deer fence, and I clambered over it and on to a Forestry road which runs through the trees of Glen Feshie, bringing me out at the field used by the Kingussie Gliding Club as a landing strip.

I stopped here for a moment and rummaged in my pack for the next map, Sheet 35 of the O.S. 1:50,000 series. A 4-mile stretch of tarmac road carried me quickly down Glen Feshie to the farm at Achlean, where I skipped across to the riverside and followed a sketchy path alongside the fast-flowing River Feshie, through another forest plantation, and into the green magnificence of upper Glen Feshie near the old bothy of Ruigh Aiteachain.

This was my stop for the night, a paradise rich in birdsong and wildlife, and luxuriant in lush vegetation. It seems that the more varied and profuse the vegetation, the richer is the birdlife, and so it is in Glen Feshie. Oyster catchers, sandpipers and curlews haunt the shingly river bank, and meadow pipits, wheatears, larks and chats are common enough in the wild extravagance of juniper and birch. Later in the evening, after I had camped and eaten, I strolled southwards by the river banks, and stood for a while watching a great herd of red deer grazing quietly by the grassy river flats. The red deer have a special significance in Feshie, as the glen has virtually been a laboratory in the science of deer management, a long-term project undertaken jointly by the Nature Conservancy Council and the Glen Feshie Estate. Coincidentally, it was near the building of Ruigh Aiteachain that the artist Edwin Landseer painted his evocative *Stag at Bay*.

I see the ridge of hinds, the steep of the sloping glen,
The wood of cuckoos at its foot,
The blue height of a thousand pines.

Ancient Gaelic poem

Cross river and follow track S.W. past Lochan an t-Stuic, through plantation, the W. into Glen Tromie, 6 miles. Cross river S.E. of Bhran Cottage and follow Allt na Feinnich S.W. over watershed and down to Loch Cuaich, 4 miles. Follow track beside aqueduct to Dalwhinnie, $4\frac{1}{2}$ miles, then walk $5\frac{1}{2}$ miles to Ben Alder Lodge on N. shore of Loch Ericht. From Ben Alder Lodge, walk due W. to Loch Pattack. Camp in vicinity. Follow footpath S.W. through Bealach Dubh, 6 miles, and down by the Uisge Labhair for 5 miles

to Loch Ossian. Take south shore track to Corrour, $4\frac{1}{2}$ miles.
Follow path on W. side of railway N.W. for $2\frac{1}{2}$ miles to Loch Treig,
then W. on track for 1 mile to Creaguaineach Lodge. Follow
footpath on N. bank of Abhainn Rath for 5 miles to Tom an Eite,
then boggy path beside Water of Nevis for 4 miles to Steall. Path
then runs through gorge to Polldubh and on to public road down
Glen Nevis to Fort William. Steall to Fort William, 8 miles.

At the head of the river flats in the south of the glen, Creag na
Caillich, the Hill of the Old Woman, stands sentinel, dividing the
upper glen in two. The Caterans' Road leaves Feshie
westwards before the Hill of the Old Woman is reached, and I
followed its course, in the company of a small herd of deer
hinds, up a steep winding path, past a small brooding lochan,
Lochan an t-Stuic, and on to the open moorland above. A small
forest plantation blocked the way westwards, but the gate
could be opened, allowing me to pass through the trees by way
of a faint path, rather than take the longer walk round the
outskirts of the plantation.

The morning had started dull and heavy, and it was warm
sweaty work with the threat of thunder hanging in the air.
Southwards, the great rolling hills of Gaick stretched away into
the distance, wide open rolling country below an even wider
cloud-tumbled sky; typical Grampian scenery. I flushed several
red grouse, who burst from the heather below my feet, their
guttural "go back, go back" taking me by surprise.

I followed the footpath which runs alongside the Allt Bhran,
past a weir and down into the birch trees which grow beside
the river in Glen Tromie. Further up the glen, Bhran Cottage lies
empty and forlorn, a haunt of sheep and curlews. A small
bridge crosses the river, and an old stalkers' path runs for a
short distance south-westwards beside the Allt na Feinnich.
This path fizzled out but I plodded on, plagued by a horde of
flies who seemed determined to dive-bomb into my eyes,
mouth and nose at any opportunity. Across the boggy
watershed I went, and on to another map, Sheet 42, Loch
Rannoch, 1:50,000.

Despite the heavy atmosphere, the ominous rumbling of distant thunder and the flies which still accompanied me, I felt some elation as I dropped down to Loch Cuaich, nestling snugly below the steep craggy slopes of Meall Cuaich. I had crossed the watershed that runs up the spine of Scotland, the historic Druim Alban, and the remainder of the walk to Fort William was now psychologically downhill. To the south-west of me, across the busy A9, the only road which I would cross in the whole of the 80 miles from Ryvoan to Fort William, lay the long silver band of Loch Ericht, stretching for some 15 miles from Dalwhinnie to the south-west, biting far into the heart of bare Rannoch Moor. It was still a good 4 miles off, so I didn't linger by Loch Cuaich. Some anglers shouted a greeting; they at least would be happy with the overcast weather. I was almost tempted to stop for a brief "crack", as backpackers and fishermen have a lot in common, sharing a deep love of these wild places. Many of them have quietly said to me, over a dram and a bothy fire, that the fish are actually one of the unimportant parts of the game. It is the solitude that many of them desire, the freedom from normal routines, the fresh tangle of wind on an upturned face, and whether one obtains these experiences from walking the hills, standing thigh deep in a Highland river, or being gently rocked in a loch-borne dinghy, is unimportant. The end product is the same, and that is surely all that matters.

An aqueduct runs from Loch Cuaich down to Dalwhinnie, part of an intricate hydro-electric system of dams, power stations, and tunnels. A plaque at the end of Loch Cuaich pronounces: "Cuaich-Seillich Tunnel, 22,310 feet, completed 1940". Loch an t-Seillich lies in Gaick, where the waters from those high hills flow through this underground tunnel to Cuaich, down the aqueduct to Dalwhinnie and Loch Ericht, which has a dam at both ends, and from Ericht's south-western end drains to Rannoch Moor, which in turn feeds the Tummel-Pitlochry systems. And I thought these hills allowed me to escape from the technology of twentieth-century man!

A friend of mine once told me a tale about his father, who worked on the building of the Cuaich-Seillich tunnel. As he was setting out to work one morning, he was stopped by a strange old man who asked him for a bite to eat. Anxious not to be late, my friend's father thought briefly of ignoring the old fellow, but there was something about his presence which made him stop, take a couple of sandwiches from his "piece", and give them to the strange old man. He was thanked, and then, almost as an afterthought, warned that under no circumstances should he go to work that day. Taken aback, he walked on, then turned round to say something, but the old man had vanished from sight. Deeply disturbed, he went home, and it was later in the day that word was brought to him that several of his close friends had been killed in a tunnel collapse!

Dalwhinnie is a bleak and desolate corner of Badenoch, with little to offer other than a good transport café, a couple of small stores, and a railway station. There is also a hotel where walking boots are frowned upon in the lounge bar! I stopped at the station and collected a parcel of fresh food which I had sent on a few days previously. Why carry it around with you when you can pick it up *en route*?

A good land rover track runs down the northern shore of Loch Ericht, an estate road which services Ben Alder Lodge, 6 miles down the lochside. Fading yellow broom fringed the side of the track, and down on the shore the odd white bleached stumps of ancient pines stood as ancient monuments of long ago, mere ghosts of their former glory. A fresh breeze was developing along the great stretch of empty water, and it cooled me nicely as I romped down those long miles, eager to reach the great empty quarter of Pattack and the Ben Alder deer forest. It was a familiar track. Many is the time I have walked briskly down here in anticipation of a couple of days on Ben Alder or on the great Aonach Beag ridge, and many is the time I have crawled back along it, cursing its long empty miles, footsore and weary. How great is the motivation of anticipation!

Nothing had changed, the great grey house standing remote

and gaunt beside its tiny bay, the great sweep of far-flung mountain and moor as the track curves due west on to the vast flats of Pattack, and frowning down on the entire scene, the black cliffs of Ben Alder and the Lancet Edge of Geal Charn, their steep slopes forming the prominent notch of the Bealach Dubh, the Black Pass, the road to the isles.

Between the alluvial flats of Loch Pattack and the peat hag-ridden moor, I managed to find a dry sheltered spot for the tent, a lovely position facing west towards the pass. There was a touch of magic in the air this evening; two white swans floated serenely on the loch, and several white horses, garrons, grazed contentedly a few yards away from the tent.

Charles Edward Stuart passed through here on his post-Culloden flight through the Highlands. Hard walking brought him from the Great Glen over the Laggan Hills and through by Loch Pattack to Ben Alder, where he was warmly greeted by Cluny MacPherson, himself a Jacobite in hiding. A rocky bower high on the south-facing slopes of Ben Alder was his erstwhile home, and it was here, in "Cluny's Cage", that Charles found shelter from his unaccustomed discomfort and continuous struggle against the elements, before word came that a French frigate awaited him off the coast of Moidart, to ferry him back to France.

Below the spot where Cluny's Cage is thought to have been, lies the pine-fringed Alder Bay, a lonely and lovely spot frequented occasionally by fishermen and hill people alike. An empty house, Ben Alder Cottage, occupies a quiet corner of the bay, believed by many to be haunted ...

Morning brought the familiar patter of rain on the flysheet. The white garrons had deserted me, no doubt preferring a dry stable somewhere to my diminishing stock of sugar cubes. The Bealach Dubh had vanished in a turmoil of cloud, and what had been a vibrant prospect of greens, browns and blacks the evening before, had, this morning, become a solemn fusion of dreichness. The perfect opportunity for a long lie.

It was after ten o'clock when I shifted myself, and my

procrastinations had paid off for once; the rain had stopped, and the clouds looked as though they were beginning to break up. A wet path ran alongside the slow-flowing Allt a'Chaoil-reidhe, past the bothy and empty lodge at Culra, and over the bumps and dips of the moraines which herald the beginnings of the Bealach Dubh. Through the great black jaws I climbed, to see a view of superb splendour unfolding. Far down the long glen in front of me lay the long waters of Loch Ossian, named after the bardic son of the great Finn McCuil, better known in Scotland as Fingal. Beyond the loch rose some of the highest hills in the west, the hills of Lochaber; the great peaks of the Mamore Forest, the Grey Corries and the Aonachs, and Ben Nevis itself. This must have been a welcome sight for the Lochaber raiders as they hurried home from their reiving, back into their own lands with their booty.

At the foot of this long glen, just east of Loch Ossian, a clan skirmish took place in the seventeenth century. Some MacDonnells of Keppoch had set out on the Caterans' Road towards Speyside, intent on a raid into Moray. They had not gone far when word was brought to them that Grants from Speyside were in fact behind them in Keppoch, "lifting" MacDonnell cattle. Infuriated, they returned without delay, caught the Grants red-handed, and killed them almost to a man. The surviving Grants, a small band of three or four, escaped, and made their way by Loch Treig to Loch Ossian where they met some strangers, to whom they confided the fact that they were being pursued, by "cursed MacDonnell heathens". Unknown to them, by doing this they instantly signed their own death warrants, for the strangers were also MacDonnells, who saved their fellow clansmen a long chase by dispatching the Grants to a quick and bloody grave.

Loch Ossian took me on to the next map, No. 41, Ben Nevis, the last map of the trip. Ossian indents the north-east corner of Rannoch Moor, a vast undulating glacial plain which forms an inhospitable expanse of peatbog and open water, a lonely place where Nature reigns supreme. The loch itself is remote, with no easy way to reach it, but it is not bleak. High mountains surround it, and the edges of the loch are softened by woods. This area is all deer forest, and you are not welcome during the shooting season from mid-August to November. I met a shepherd on the track which runs along the south side of the loch. His black and white collie bitch trotted along behind him, her tiny black shiny nose wearing a dent behind her master's knee! We remarked on the weather, and he asked me how far I was going. When I told him Fort William, he told me to keep an eye open for a white deer which had recently been spotted in the Creaguaineach area near Loch Treig. "It'll no live long I'm thinking," he said. "The older stags'll kill it off as it's no one o' them." I promised to keep a look out, and we said goodbye, he off eastwards to the Lodge, with the long striding gait of hill shepherds, the hardiest bunch of all.

A youth hostel sits on a tiny peninsula at the western end of the loch, a hostel of the type which is disappearing, sadly. A wooden shack of a building, it has an atmosphere which is peculiar to this type of accommodation; the reek of the red-hot kitchen stove, the steamed up windows, the boiling pots and pans, and the conversation in a dozen languages as young people of different backgrounds and creeds mix together in the relaxing beauty of a magnificent setting. How different it is in "modern" youth hostels, where so many are intent on "doing" Scotland in a week, and spend their evenings huddled over a pool table or around a television set, where once they would have relaxed with a song, a joke, and a tune on the "moothie". Changed days indeed. A Y.H.A. official recently told me that modern youth was more "sophisticated". God help us all. Thankfully, the Scottish Youth Hostel Association are striving to meet the cost of keeping up these little gems like Ossian, Glen Affric, Carn Dearg and one or two others, for those who enjoy meeting like-minded souls in an atmosphere of friendship and informality.

A mile from the hostel lies the railway station at Corrour, on the Glasgow to Fort William line or, as it is known, the West

Highland Line, possibly the most scenic train ride in the country. A path follows the line north-westwards to the southern shores of Loch Treig, a long 6-mile trough hemmed in on both sides by 3,000-foot mountains. The scenery hereabouts is more bleak than beautiful, with the rubbly shoreline of the loch, caused by the raising and lowering of the water line, looking very much the worse for wear. The waters of Treig help power the aluminium factory at Fort William, which seems rather a strange fact since Fort William is over 15 miles away, but a long tunnel was burrowed in 1929 from here, through part of Ben Nevis, and down to the aluminium works. When it was finished it was the first tunnel of its type in the world.

Heading away from the rueful shores, I passed another empty house, Creaguaineach Lodge, crossed a bridge over the rushing waters of the Abhainn Rath, which has its source high in the bowels of the Grey Corries, just east of Ben Nevis. A small ledge high above the track, surrounded by bright patches of chickweed wintergreen, yellow primroses, dwarf and butterwort, the insectivorous plant of moist ground, looked like an ideal spot for the night, and a bubbling of pure stream water nearby convinced me. Up went the tent, on went the stove, and I settled in for the night. It wasn't until mid-way through the evening that I remember what the shepherd by Loch Ossian had told me about the white deer, so, in the falling darkness, I wandered up the hill behind me for a look around. There was no deer to be seen at all, but I was rewarded none the less by the sight of a red fox. Its sudden movement just caught my attention in the dimness, and it stopped and stared at me quite unconcerned, twitching its ears and nose, before trotting off in that sly way that foxes have.

The final 17 or so miles to Fort William are delightful, and contrast strongly with the rich pastoral scenery of the meadows and woods below Staoineag, and the bare wetlands of Tom an Eite, the watershed between Loch Treig and Glen Nevis.

I moved off early to a rousing chorus of stonechats, pipits, lapwings and tits, with a family of dippers joining me in the gentle stravaig alongside the Abhainn Rath, through glorious green meadows alive with primroses and harebells, the Scottish bluebell. This does not seem like a Highland landscape, it is too gentle, with the river meandering slowly around the vibrant green meadows, shaded by birch and rowan, surrounded by gentle slopes; but the pastoral gentleness does not last long. Above the meadows, the river takes on its Highland aspect again, and comes rushing through the narrow gorge with desperation and rush. Sandpipers and greenshank called as I passed the bothy at Staoineag on the opposite side of the river, with the outline of the Mamores and the Ben pulling me onwards like some massive magnet.

The old house at Luibelt lay silent and desolate, even the protecting clutch of pines beside it failing to save it from the decaying ferocity of the winter winds. The ubiquitous sheep graze here in their hundreds, sharing the rich feeding with the occasional herd of deer. This is an open landscape, and the pull of the mountains is all around; on the left, the great ridges of the Mamores, and on the right, the Grey Corries, the bulk of the Aonachs, and the bald smooth pate of Ben Nevis dominating all.

The rough path on the north bank of the Abhainn Rath at Luibelt has to be swopped for the one on the south bank, and there is no bridge, it means a ford and probably wet feet. It doesn't really matter all that much though, because a couple of miles further on lies Tom an Eite, one of the boggiest and wettest places that I know. From here down to Steall, the Water of Nevis kept me company, growing very quickly from a mere boggy puddle at Tom an Eite, to the raging torrent of gargantuan proportions and power as it roars its way through the gorge from Steall to upper Polldubh. Steall itself is a fine spot, and a constant source of surprise to those who follow the path above the wooded ravine from the car park at Polldubh. From a jumble of fallen rocks and boulders one comes across a

scene of utter tranquillity, despite the crashing and thundering
of the huge "White Mare's Tail" waterfall which drops down
sheer from Coire a Mhail. This shady and peaceful place is not
without sadness though, for a few years ago, when the cottage
at Lower Steall (nowadays a climbers' hut) was a croft, the
crofter was cutting hay on the meadow opposite the house,
when his wife sent their young daughter down to summon her
father for a meal. She slipped while attempting to cross the
fast-flowing river, and was carried away by the current. Her
body was found five miles downstream. A wire hawser bridge
now spans the bridge at the spot where the young girl went in,
and I stopped for a while to watch heavily laden climbers
negotiate the tricky obstacle course of a bridge. It takes a brave
heart to cross that bridge when the river is running full, and
more than one climber has fallen in here to his cost.

Below Steall, as I have mentioned, the Water of Nevis takes
on its role as thundering cataract, as it flows from the flats and
gouges its way through and down a tight narrow gorge. Huge
smoothed boulders fill the deep river bed, and the waters take
absolutely no notice of them, crashing, surging, rumbling and
roaring over, below and past them, in a mad race to reach the
bottom of the glen and the open obscurity of Loch Linnhe.

I enjoyed the walk which slopes down beside the gorge,
hugging the wet rocky walls, in places eroded by the tread of a
thousand boot soles, and exposed to the crashing waters
below, a path which has been likened by more than one writer
to a high-level Himalayan trail. It wasn't long before I reached
the car park at Polldubh, and the start of a 5-mile stretch of
tarmac road to Fort William. But this is not an anticlimax,
tarmac road or not. The thundering river makes a good
companion, and the gnarled pines which fringe the road are old
and proud, so full of character. The glen floor is well covered in
birch and pine, and the road twists and undulates its way
northwards, past the youth hostel, the campsite, the end of the
Glasgow to Fort William West Highland Way, and the end of
this walk. No doubt the fat Moray cattle were a few pounds

slimmer by the time they were allowed to graze freely on the meadows of Glen Nevis and the surrounding glens, well nigh exhausted as they must have been after their unaccustomed run along the Rathad nam Meirleach.

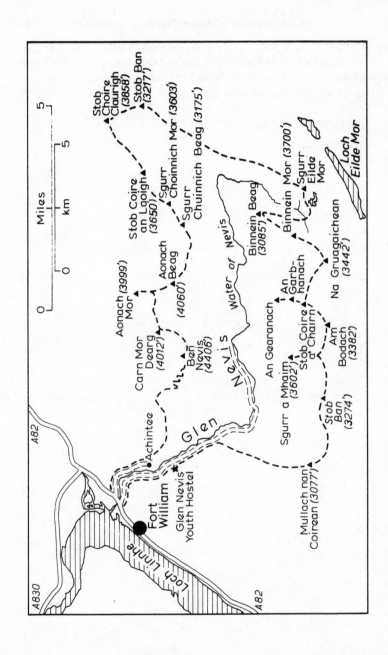

ROUTE 3: GLEN NEVIS HIGH-LEVEL CIRCUIT

About 40 miles and 20,000 feet of ascent. A two-camp high-level mountain walk. A round trip from Ben Nevis to the Aonachs and the Grey Corries, traversing the whole of the Mamore Ridge westwards back to Glen Nevis.

Map required: O.S. 1:50,000 Second Series. Sheet 41.

From Achintee Farm, 1¾ miles S.E. of Fort William, take tourist path to summit of Ben Nevis, 5 miles. Follow marker posts curving S.E. then N.E. to Carn Mor Dearg Arete, 1 mile. Climb to summit of Carn Mor Dearg. Descend slopes due E. to bealach, ¼ mile, then climb E., then N. to Aonach Mor, 1 mile. Retrace steps to bealach between Aonach Mor and Aonach Beag, and ascend the latter, S.S.E. Follow line of cliffs S.E., and work your way carefully down through the crags of bealach W.S.W. of Sgurr Chuinnich Beag. Camp.

Solo mountain backpacking tends to be frowned upon by the various outdoors authorities as an exceedingly risky business, and I suppose morally they are quite correct. An unforeseen tumble, a wrenched ankle, or even something as simple and mundane as an upset stomach, could have, to say the least, uncomfortable results, but mountain walking is generally accepted as a risk activity, even if nowadays, thanks to first-class clothing and equipment, the risk is small. To be more accurate, the risk is small to experienced walkers, and beginners should always go with an experienced companion.

Fifteen years and more of mountain walking qualified me for this particular ploy, and since I knew these hills well, I had the added advantage of knowledge of the topography. To complete a walk like this on one's own, several things are necessary; the correct lightweight equipment, as a heavily laden mountain backpacker is a slow and cumbersome, and usually unhappy, creature; the ability to use that equipment; a tolerable degree of physical fitness; and most important of all, a clear and honest understanding of one's own limitations. If you have the slightest doubt on the negative side of this understanding, go with an experienced companion. I put the emphasis on the word experienced, as two incompetent backpackers are a damned sight more dangerous than one!

Fort William is on the railway line from the south, although backpackers using this form of transport will have a 3-mile walk to the start of the route at Achintee Farm in Glen Nevis, south-east of the town. I started from Glen Nevis Youth Hostel, a couple of miles further up the glen, where the well-worn path strikes up the boggy lower slopes of Ben Nevis, and meets the Achintee track after a quarter of a mile or so. One of the golden rules of travelling alone is to leave an accurate route plan with someone, with an E.T.A. of your finish, so that in the event of your having an accident, the rescue authorities can be notified if you don't turn up at the specified time. I left a route card with the Warden of the Youth Hostel.

Travelling comfortably over high mountains like the ones on this route, means travelling light, and I carried with me a pack of slightly over 20 pounds; a lightweight tent of just over four pounds, an extremely lightweight gas stove, and enough dried food to sustain me for three days.

I had been around this circuit before, and judged it to be the finest sustained high-level trip I had done. Philip Tranter, son of novelist Nigel Tranter, had once waltzed round this same route inside 24 hours, a seemingly astonishing time which paled to insignificance as a feat of endurance when it was repeated a few years later by a lady in her mid fifties! So much for the weaker sex! I had toyed with the idea of trying to repeat this performance, but, in a fit of inverted competitiveness, decided to wander round at ease, and enjoy the hills to the full. Whilst many feel that treating the hills as a race track is some lower form of sacrilege, there is a great deal of satisfaction to be gained from the purely physical challenge of pitting your strength and fitness against the rough and rugged terrain of the mountains. If it is borne in mind that you are not competing against the mountains, but against yourself, then moving fast in the hills can offer a tremendous opportunity for self-revelation. On this particular trip I wanted a therapy rather than a test, a reward, if you like, rather than a trial.

The track from Achintee to the summit of Ben Nevis, unless it is your first time and you harbour a strong desire to climb Britain's highest mountain by its quickest route, probably falls into the dull category. The mountain itself, from the south, is definitely dull, and hides its real sensations in the clench of its north-east-facing Coire Leis, the 2000-foot-high barricade of cliffs and crags which offers the finest snow- and ice-climbing in Britain. Unfortunately, the vast majority of "Ben Nevis Baggers" never sees this side of the mountain; to obtain a glimpse of the true character of the hill, one must combine the ascent of the Ben with that of Carn Mor Dearg which lies to the north. We shall, in fact, be doing so on this route.

The Achintee track runs for about five miles to the summit of the Ben, a long relentless pull from just above sea level to 4406 feet, the highest point above the level of the sea in all of Britain. The track first of all winds round the shoulder of Meall an t-Suidhe, the Ben's westerly neighbour, and then, by a series of zigzags, makes its way up the steep western shoulder of the stony slopes to the broad summit plateau. In summer, you are rarely alone. I passed a steady procession of walkers making their way to the top; well-equipped hill walkers, balaclava-clad and earnest; a young family, the youngest of whom was perched precariously on the shoulders of his father; an older couple, welly booted and carrying umbrellas; and a squad of orange-cagouled soldiers who were obviously, by their grunts and curses, not enjoying themselves one little bit.

Such is the magnetic pull of Britain's highest hill!

Whippet-lean fell runners annually flee up and down the mountain from Fort William and back in the course of the Ben Nevis Hill Race. The fastest time of just under ninety minutes is rarely believed by mere mortals. Laden backpackers can regard three and a half hours to the summit as fairly steady going.

As I reached the top of the zigzags, the mist and cloud which seems to be a permanent fixture obliterated any view that I might have hoped for. As you would expect, the view, in clear conditions, is an extensive one ranging from Torridon to Ireland, and from the Hebrides to the blue Cairngorms. Closer at hand, to the south, the pointed fangs of the Glencoe Hills and the Mamores form impressive barriers, and to the west Loch Linnhe and Loch Eil stretch their long fingers seawards.

When the cloud is down, great care is needed, as many of the deep-set gullies of the precipitous north-east face extend far into the summit plateau. When they are fringed by broad cornices of snow, as they are until well into the summer, take extra care, as these shapely waves of wind-blown snow are often dangerously delicate and will break away if any weight is applied to them.

The summit of the Ben is a largish plateau of scree and stones, once described by a Scots writer as "the highest midden in Britain". An orange-painted Nissen hut decorates the top, and no doubt serves its purpose as an emergency shelter well. Aesthetically it leaves a lot to be desired. The actual cairn is like no other in Scotland, decorated (desecrated perhaps?) by a number of totally irrelevant plaques bearing remembrance to any number of causes from the survivors of Hiroshima, to a crudely painted "Wullie wis here, August 1979". The ruins of another building, the old Observatory, bear testament to the brave men who worked here at the end of the last century collecting and collating meteorological data. The old records show how the name Ben Nevis is often thought to mean the "venomous mountain"; it has a mean annual rainfall of 157 inches, with a maximum of 240 inches; a mean monthly temperature half a degree below freezing; snow can fall on any day of the year, and the permanent winter fall often begins in October! The summit has an average of 261 gales each year, many of which reach hurricane force, often with gusts of 150 m.p.h. in winter. Warm clothing is advised. "Venomous mountain" seems somehow more appropriate than the other possible explanation of the name Ben Nevis: the Mountain of Heaven. If Heaven is like that you can keep it!

I didn't linger on top, it was far too chilly for hanging around, even in July, and the grey cloud which covered everything was damp. I scurried off towards the scree slopes which lead in a south-easterly direction towards the Carn Mor Dearg Arete, and better backpacking hills. Care was needed in the mist to find the correct route, as a course held for too long to the east can lead one into difficulties at the top of the often frozen slopes which drop off into upper Coire Leis. Further down, as the gradient becomes easier, it is equally as important not to wander too far to the south, as you would then find yourself in Coire Eoghainn. A line of posts, with warning notices, has been erected to help you keep the true line. The highest of these signs is about 130 yards from the summit cairn on a magnetic bearing of 128 degrees, and the posts follow at intervals of 20 to 30 yards. I would not advise backpackers to follow this route to Carn Mor Dearg Arete in winter though, unless they were experienced winter campaigners kitted out with sharp crampons and an ice axe. The slopes thaw and freeze in quick succession and often form great boiler-plate slabs of iron-hard ice. In these conditions the only safe way back to sea level is back the way you came, over the summit and down the Achintee track.

The Carn Mor Dearg Arete (horrible foreign name) leads you on a rocky tightrope to the summit of Carn Mor Dearg. It's an exciting prospect, the great airy sweep of the graceful curve which forms the south-west wall of Coire Leis. Again, care is needed, and laden backpackers will quickly realize the advantage of travelling light. You may have left some of the luxuries of camp life at home, but you will be glad you are not carrying the extra weight on delicate little traverses like this one. As I crossed the Arete, whose crest is still a lofty 3478 feet, I came below the cloud and enjoyed the views of the great glistening crags and cliffs vanishing into a block of cloud above. These cliffs are the domain of the climbers, boasting some of the traditional classics of Scottish rock and ice.

I lingered for a while on Carn Mor Dearg's summit cairn, hoping, in vain, for the cloud to rise a little. It was only 2 p.m. and I looked forward to ambling slowly over Aonach Mor and Aonach Beag, the two bulky hills which rise due east of Carn Mor Dearg. These hills are something of a Gaelic anomaly, since Aonach Mor, which means "the big ridge", is at 3999 feet lower than Aonach Beag, the "little ridge", at 4060 feet. It only proves that the people who named these hills were less interested in the actual heights of the hills, but judged them as big and small from their mass. In this respect, Aonach Beag is certainly larger. The height and numbers game is a comparatively modern phenomenon, and just shows that even self-confessed non-competitive hill types are often motivated by ticking off the Munros in their books. It's a crazy game, since there are numerous superb peaks which fail to make the required 3000-foot line. One only has to think of such hills as the Cobbler, Stac Polly, Suilven or the Arran ridges to realize how crazy we are. But, for the sake of achieving some sort of standard, we strive on regardless.

I ate some chocolate, and gave up on the cloud clearing, before moving off down the east ridge to the high bealach below Aonach Mor. Another short climb of about 700 feet, and a south-eastwards traverse on the flanks, took me to the saddle between the two Aonachs. I dumped my pack beside a prominent boulder, and floated up Aonach Mor unladen. This summit ridge is gravelly, with long steep drops on either side. I was back in the cloud again, the wraith-like fingers of damp hurrying me along, no lingering, just a touch of the cairn, and a back track to the bealach again. I was anxious to get over Aonach Beag, a tricky hill in the mist, as quickly as possible. It seemed odd that despite my promises of a relaxed easy stroll over these hills, I was hurrying myself along, a bit uptight and nervy. I collected my pack, and climbed to the tiny cairn which marks the top of Aonach Beag. I had climbed this hill several times before, but always in good weather, and now that I was here in thick cloud, the words of Hamish Brown kept floating through my mind. In his book *Hamish's Mountain Walk*, he advised, "This is not a good area to wander about in if there is thick cloud, not unless you have a parachute." Steep cliffs fall sharply away to the north-east into the An Aghaidh Gharbh, the rounded dome of the summit area is conducive to becoming lost, as several folk have found to their cost. I relaxed a lot more once I made my way alongside the cliff tops (not so easy in mist if they are corniced), to a subsidiary top at the eastern end of the ridge, and managed to make my way carefully and slowly down through the steep rocky slopes to the high bealach below Sgurr Choinnich Beag. If you feel at all hesitant about negotiating these steep slopes down to the bealach, or if snow conditions make this an undesirable descent route, swallow your pride and follow the slopes of Aonach Beag in a S.S.E. direction to the outlying top of Sgurr a'Bhuic, below which an easier corrie leads to safe ground. It means that you will have to traverse around the slopes of Sgurr a'Bhuic to climb back up to the Choinnich Beag bealach, but what is a little extra time and effort if it is safer?

Although only a little after 4 p.m., I decided to stop on the flattish bealach below Sgurr Choinnich Beag for the night. The next stretch of the walk is a high-level ridge of some 5 miles along the crests of the Grey Corries, and I didn't really see much point in bashing along them in cloud. Besides, there is something truly relaxing about festering around in a high-level camp on a long summer evening, too high for the midges, and too low for the cloud, drinking endless brews and reading a book. It makes you feel as though you own the damned place. I wandered down the slope for a couple of hundred feet and found some water, then cooried doon on a small flat square of turf surrounded by the fading remnants of patches of moss campion. With some rocks for a kitchen, and the soft springy grass for a bed, I had a view both north and south instead of confining walls. All the mountains I could see had their heads chopped off by the heavy grey cloud base; Binnein Beag and Mor, the start of the long Mamore chain, my hills for the day after tomorrow, and, beyond, the long wall of the Aonach Eagach ridge which forms the northern jaws of Glencoe. To the north stretched the great wilderness of mountains beyond the Great Glen, the Loch Arkaig group, the Quoich Hills, Affric, Kintail and Torridon, a myriad of mountains to excite any hill lover.

Traverse ridge of Sgurr Choinnich Beag, Sgurr Choinnich Mor, Stob Coire Easain, Stob Coire an Loaigh (the 3659-foot top unnamed on map), and N.E. to Stob Choire Claurigh, 4 miles. Descend S.S.E. towards Stob Ban, and ascend slopes of same, 1 mile. Descend slopes of Stob Ban in a S.W. direction into Coire Rath, and follow Allt Coire Rath to Tom an Eite, $2\frac{3}{4}$ miles. Climb slopes of Meall Coire na h-Achlais to the S.S.E., 1 mile and then follow broad ridge S.W. to summit of Sgurr Eilde Mor. Drop down prominent nose S.W. to lochan. Camp. Take stalkers' path which lies N.W. of the lochan in a winding N.W. direction for $1\frac{1}{2}$ miles to the W. slopes of Binnein Beag. Climb to summit of Binnein Beag. Drop back to lochan below the hill in a S.S.W. direction and ascend Binnein Mor by way of its N.E. corrie. Follow ridge from summit S. to the unnamed top, $\frac{1}{2}$ mile, then S.W. to Na Gruagaichean, $\frac{1}{2}$ mile. Cross N.W. top of Na Gruagaichean and follow prominent ridge N.W. for $1\frac{1}{2}$ miles to Stob Coire a Chairn. Ascend An Garbhanach and An Gearanach in N., and return to Stob Coire a Chairn the same way. Take ridge S.W. to steep screes of Am Bodach, 1 mile, then W.N.W. to Sgurr an Iubhair, unnamed on map, $\frac{3}{4}$ mile. Leave pack at cairn and cross Devil's Ridge to the N. to Sgurr a Mhaim, returning to Sgurr an Iubhair the same way. An easy track avoids the worst (or best?) of the ridge on the east side of the rocks, Follow ridge which winds gently W. to Stob Ban,

$1\frac{1}{4}$ miles, then winding ridge N., then W., and S.W. to 900-metre unnamed top, then N.W. to Mullach nan Coirean. Descend to Glen Nevis by N. ridge of Mullach, by Sgurr Chalum and forest fire breaks to Youth Hostel in Glen Nevis.

I was up and away by 7 a.m., an early rise being the great advantage of an early night. The cloud had dropped during the night, enveloping my tiny tent in a damp grey shroud, but, as I lay in my sleeping-bag in the half-conscious state which waking brings, it miraculously lifted before my eyes, like a dream, and patches of blue sky were quickly becoming larger through great rents in the sky. No time to linger now that there was a prospect of early morning views, the finest of all.

The Grey Corries have often been likened to huge heaps, a slanderous and unfair description. They are marvellous hills to walk, much of the time on good quartzy rock. It is the ash-grey colour of this rock which often leads people to think that the hills are capped in unseasonal snow, hence the popular name for the ridge, the Grey Corries. The ridge itself is long and switchbacked, meandering its way over three Munros: Sgurr Choinnich Mor, 3603 feet, Stob Coire an Laoigh, 3659 feet, and not named on the O.S. 1:50,000 map, and Stob Choire Claurigh, 3858 feet. An outlier to the east, Stob Ban, 3217 feet, is also a Munro. Altogether there are seven tops on the ridge, which, with the inclusion of Stob Ban, make a memorable day's walking.

The first two tops, Sgurr Choinnich Beag and Mor, the small mossy peak and the big mossy peak, give a good warm-up to the day's exertions. Beag presents no problems at all, with the going easy over short brown turf. The sun was now bursting through, the air was brisk and the colours were beginning to give those magical changes an emphasis and intensity which can only be found on Highland hills. Sgurr Choinnich Mor ahead heralded the start of the ridge proper, and as I clambered noisily down its eastern slopes on a scree-strewn path, through interesting peaks and great holes in the quartzy strata, the great swing of the ridge stretched out before me in a long muscular arm.

As a ridge walk it is easy, with few obstacles to cause concern to the backpacker; but the views of the ridge itself, and of its near and far neighbours, the dazzling effects of the sun squinting off the snow-white crests, the exquisite formation of the graceful curves of the corrie rims, and the breathtaking impression of a great height above Glen Nevis in the south and Glen Spean in the north, make the ridge a fabulous expedition.

It is amazing how the spirits rise and fall with the cloud level. The previous day I felt apprehension on Aonach Beag; today I felt a great uplifting as I wandered along the narrowing ridge over small scree and rocks, spotting familiar peaks in all directions. A slight breeze was cool enough to be comfortable, and I was oblivious to the weight of my pack as I strode from top to top. Stob Coire Easain came and went, and still the ridge flowed on in undulating waves. A turn to the south-east gave me the unnamed Munro which in fact is Stob Coire an Laoigh, the Hill of the Corrie of the Calves, and going over the subsidiary tops towards Stob Choire Claurigh I met my first walkers of the day, a couple from England who had bothyed at Staoineag near Loch Treig and had just climbed on to the ridge from Tom an Eite far below. I was glad that I had camped high the night before as the lady proceeded to show me her badly midge-bitten arms and legs. The poor devils had been driven from their sleeping bags at some ungodly hour, and as quickly as they could, climbed up into a breeze where they were freed from the ravages of the tiny terrors. I, rather patronizingly, commiserated, and made a mental note to camp high again that night. Off they went westwards, scratching, to finish at Steall in Glen Nevis, and I stopped for a short break. Below me, tiny glaciated lochans sparkled deep blue in the sun, a herd of deer moved like a cloud shadow on the slopes below, and from somewhere much closer, a lark twittered excitedly. Across Coire Rath, the afterthought of Stob Ban looked comfortingly small in comparison to these giants of the Grey Corries. I had made good time on the ridges, and there and then decided that after reaching Stob Choire Claurigh, I would traverse Stob Ban, and wander up the slopes of Sgurr Eilde Mor which lay across the glen to the south. Just as Stob Ban is an afterthought to the Grey Corries, so Sgurr Eilde Mor is something of an afterthought to the mighty Mamore ridge. I knew from past experience of a delectable campsite beside a high level lochan on the southern flanks of the hill, which would not only give me another campsite, but an easy start to the Binneins, Mor and Beag, the real start to the Mamore ridge, the next morning. That would give me 12 miles and about 4500 feet climbing for the day, nothing too exhausting.

Stob Choire Claurigh is the highest of the Grey Corries. From its summit, I gazed back along the ash-grey switchbacks to the great seamed cliffs of the Aonachs, and beyond them, in all its elevated glory, Ben Nevis itself, its rounded top now clear of cloud and its black cliffs as awesome as ever. Clambering over blocks and boulders of quartzite I felt it strange to be climbing down to collect the Munro of Stob Ban. An unfamiliar sensation, but a nice one at this time of day. A herd of deer scattered to the winds as I galloped down the grassy slopes, past the little lochan on the bealach, over a bump, and on to the slopes of Stob Ban. To the east lay the outlying tops of Stob Coire Easain and Stob a Choire Mheadhoin, separated by the deep-set trough of the Lairig Leacach which runs south-eastwards from Spean Bridge to the head of Loch Treig. This through route was often used in days gone by as a drove road, for driving great herds of cattle to the great cattle trysts in the south. Today, it is a useful route for walkers who want to reach these eastern Grey Corries. A motorable road runs from Corriechoille near Spean Bridge to an old bothy at the foot of the north-east ridge of Stob Ban.

Rather than make my way down to the glen over the intervening hump of Meall a Bhuirich, I followed the broad grassy slopes south-westwards into Coire Rath, and followed its stream, the Allt Coire Rath, to the humpy moraines of Tom an Eite, which must be one of the wettest and boggiest inland areas in Scotland. It would have been nice to stop hereabouts for a bit and a brew, but I couldn't find a dry place to sit! The boggy morass quivered as I tentatively tiptoed from tussock to tussock, and, almost inevitably, it wasn't long before I went in up to the knees. Oh well, once your feet are sodden you tend to throw caution to the winds, so I just spludged on through the bogs, and right through the infant Abhainn Rath which has its source high up in Coire Rath below Stob Choire Claurigh. At least the clean water cleaned the peat and mud from my legs! I once passed through here in winter, and the ground was so icy the whole area was like a vast skating rink. It was so slippy I had to stop and put on crampons to stop myself slithering around like a cat on ice.

To the south, the long whale-back ridge of Sgurr Eilde Mor rises from its prominent subsidiary, Meall Coire na h'Achlais, in a very gentle curve to its broad flat top, 3279 feet above sea level. Its easy slopes and long broad ridge present no problems to the backpacker, although the descent from the summit into Coire an Lochain, where I intended camping was steep with loose rock and slippy screes. Some measure of care is required here.

The lochan, or more correctly, the large lochan and its two or three smaller dependents, snuggle cosily in the high flat bealach between the steep crumbly southern slopes of Sgurr Eilde Mor and the even steeper black crags of Sgurr Eilde Beag, which is actually more of a subsidiary top of Binnein Mor, than a top in its own right. A herd of about twenty deer bounded off towards Binnein Beag in the north-west as they heard me slither down the screes, and some gulls screeched noisily and raucously above the loch, angry at my noisy intrusion. Just as I had pitched the tent and was organizing the stove for a brew, a long mournful wail sounded from the opposite side of the lochan. It was a long rising high-pitched cry which brought a shiver running down my spine, the sombre cry of a diver, probably a red-throated diver. It was an eerie sound in the stillness of the evening, a true cry of solitude and wilderness. I sat outside the tent sipping hot lemon tea, but I think I gained more sustenance from drinking in the atmosphere around me. A plover cried its melancholy "T-lui, t-lui" from nearby, and the diver wailed again, further away this time. The stream further down the corrie contributed a background percussion, and the gently lapping waters of the lochan pulsed quietly and steadily. This, above all else, is the great advantage of solo backpacking. You may miss points that an observant partner may notice, and you may if you are honest, occasionally feel yourself to be a lonely and deserted being through which the winds of night sigh dolefully, but all the occasional pangs of separation from loved ones are a small price to pay for being infinitely more receptive to the moods of nature. The wilderness cried out in all its quiet beauty, and I went off to bed with the sound of it ringing in my ears.

During the night, the wind rose and chased off the quietness. It turned out a breezy morning, but thankfully clear. I packed the gear, now very light indeed since I had eaten almost all the food, and found and followed the stalkers' path which runs round the western slopes of the bealach. This is a good path, and leads to the small lochan which nestles below the symmetrical cone shape of Binnein Beag. I left my pack beside the lochan, and climbed the steep shingly quartzite to the summit cairn. Binnein Beag (3083 feet), like Stob Ban, looks too wee to be a Munro in comparison to its bigger neighbours, but being out on a limb, offers good views to some of the other Mamores. Compared to the gentle Grey Corries, the Mamores are a tough bunch, with narrow airy ridges, vast wind-scoured corries, and in general, more demanding walking. They offer some of the finest continuous high-level ridge wandering in the country. They also offer ten Munros, a great temptation and incentive to Munro baggers, but you have to work hard for them. The narrow rocky crests demand careful attention and concentration, and one or two short sections of ridge require the use of the hands, but they are still walkers' hills; it's just that they demand a little more respect than most other hills.

I descended to the lochan again, and collected the pack. A steep and rocky north ridge leads to the narrow summit ridge of Binnein Mor, thrust up by steep-sided flanks. This, at 3700 feet, is the highest of the Mamores, and it is a superb mountain. Views today extended from Cruachan in the south west to the Torridons in the north. The actual summit of Binnein Mor is a little way out on a limb from the main ridge, and I enjoyed the breezy half mile or so southwards to gain the main Mamore ridge. The cool breeze that blew whipped away any warmth that the sun offered, and I had to step it out briskly to keep warm. The ridge, which had broadened out on Binnein Mor's south summit, soon narrowed again on the approach to the twin-topped Na Gruagaichean, the Maiden, at 3442 feet. The Scottish Mountaineering Club guidebook to the area describes this hill as a rather featureless mountain, but in my humble opinion it is a fine one, with its two paps a quarter of a mile or so apart. The southern top is the higher, with a drop of about two hundred feet before you begin climbing the narrow ridge to the second top.

Na Gruagaichean sits perched high above the village of Kinlochleven in the south, and allows good views over the Devil's Staircase to Rannoch Moor and the steep-sided flanks of mighty Buachaille Etive Mor. I once climbed the Maiden as a climax to a week's walk on the West Highland Way, which runs for almost a hundred miles from Glasgow to Fort William. The "official" finish to the route is unimaginative and mundane from Kinlochleven to Fort William, so I finished on a high, literally, note by climbing the Maiden and the rest of the Mamore ridge. My pack was fairly heavy after being out for a week, and I had to struggle a bit, but it was well worth the extra effort; after a week of walking low-level tracks, I was desperate to get to grips with a mountain!

The next top of the ridge to the north-west is Stob Coire a Chairn, which is not named on the 1:50,000 map. The main ridge swings south-west from Stob Coire a Chairn towards Am

Bodach, the Old Man, but two outliers to the north, An Garbhanach and An Gearanach, the rough and the short ridge, provide an exhilarating packless scramble. Both these tops are given as 3200 feet, and I didn't know which was the Munro, although most people climb both anyway. The ridge between the two is tightrope stuff, a heady ridge with steep grassy slopes falling away on either side. I enjoyed the exposure, but found the gusty wind a little tricky in places, especially on the steepish rocks which drop off from An Garbhanach on to the ridge proper.

The next Munro on the ridge, Am Bodach, 3382 feet, sits proudly at the head of Coire a'Mhail, directly above the hut down at Steall. A stalkers' track skirts across the lower slopes of the hill to reach the main ridge at Sgurr an Iubhair further on, but I climbed up through the rough broken crags through a succession of loose scree gullies to gain the summit. It was worth it to get the good airy view across to Ben Nevis and the graceful curving sweep of the Carn Mor Dearg Arete. The ridge then runs easily down to a 2800-foot saddle, giving views across to Stob Ban and Mullach nan Coirean in the distance. To the south the blue waters of Loch Leven glinted in the sun, and the long barrier of the Aonach Eagach ridge culminating in the rounded wart of the Pap of Glencoe was backed by the peaks of the Bidean nam Bian massif. The ridge began rising again over white screes to Sgurr an Iubhair, the Peak of the Yew Tree, again not named on the map. This peak, like Stob Coire a Chairn, has a northern outlier which is of Munro status, Sgurr a Mhaim, the hill which totally dominates Glen Nevis when seen from the lower reaches of the glen. Like its eastern neighbours Gearanach and Garbhanach, it lies at the end of a very narrow ridge, alarmingly nicknamed the Devil's Ridge. In winter, under snow and ice conditions, it is a formidable proposition, but in summer it is no worse than the Gearanach ridge: not technically difficult, but requiring a cool head nevertheless! The S.M.C. guide describes it as an "exhilarating walk", although another account I once read, written by a lady renowned for a loathing for and fear of tight ridges, described it thus: "The slightest stumble or mis-step anywhere sends you to the high drop ... with all hell gaping below. It is narrow and inexorable; to the walker it is fraught with menace." I would humbly submit that it is a marvellous place, and not to be missed, especially as you can leave your pack by the cairn on Sgurr an Iubhair and cross the ridge unladen. Two thirds of the way across, a series of rocks form the crest of the ridge, with a safe path running around them on the eastern side. Without the disadvantage of a pack slung around my shoulders, I scrambled my way over the top of the rocks, elementary rock climbing, and reached the slopes to Sgurr a Mhaim twittering in delight. It was so good I went back the same way.

Collecting my pack, I calmed down sufficiently to cram some chocolate and raisins into my mouth. It was too cold to linger, and I would have liked to drop down to the high lochan which lies slightly west of the Iubhair ridge for a brew up. This is a favourite lunch place of mine, for eating the "piece" and enjoying the long views down the length of green Glen Nevis, the tiny cars the size of ants crawling along the curvy glen road.

I was beginning to feel tired. All the Mamore Munros in a day is a hefty walk, and I still had two to go. Stob Ban, a beautiful hill, in a shapely peak of predominantly ash-grey quartz, hence its name, the White Hill. I struggled up its rocky ridge slowly and deliberately, fully aware that the last Munro of the day, Mullach nan Coirean, was still a long way off. At the summit, I took a five-minute break, and gazed back along the ridge eastwards. Binnein Mor stood out impressively above the others; it seemed a long way back. I was homeward bound now, and I headed off northwards, then due west along the Stob Ban ridge until I came across the lip of the huge eastern corrie of the last Munro. I followed the cliff edge round past the south-east top, and then a descent, a re-ascent to the broad flat summit ridge. No sharp conical peak here, but a flat plateau-like summit, difficult to navigate in mist. The wind was really picking up now, and every step was becoming a battle on the exposed summit ridge. Three thousand feet below lay Glen Nevis and home, and rather than struggle down the steep slopes directly below me, I followed the well-defined north ridge towards the minor top of Sgurr Chalum. The easy and gentle sloping ridge was, somewhat surprisingly, a joy to wander down. No leg-jarring descent here at the end of a hard day, but an easy and relaxing finale to what had been a marvellous round. I followed one of the forest fire breaks through the plantation and very quickly found myself back on the Glen Nevis road, a mile or so south of the Youth Hostel where I had left my car.

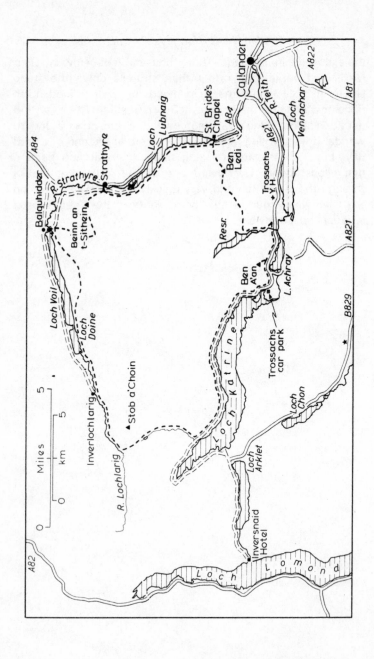

ROUTE 4: FOLLOWING THE GREGORACH

About 58 miles. An easy two-camp historical walk following the route of the Fiery Cross (as described by Sir Walter Scott) through the Trossachs.

Maps required: O.S. 1:50,000 Second Series. Sheets 56, 57.

Leave pier at the Trossachs and walk S.E. swinging N.E. on minor road to the junction with A821, 1 mile. Continue E. on A821, past Trossachs Hotel to Brig o' Turk, $2\frac{1}{4}$ miles. Follow minor road N.W. from Brig o' Turk, but don't follow it all the way to the dam. Three-quarters of a mile from Brig o' Turk the road splits, and our route goes right, and climbs to the east of the Glen Finglas Reservoir, to a point beside a small wood. Strike N.E. up the open hillside beyond the wood, and follow the long knobbly ridge over Stuc Odhar to Ben Ledi, 2882 feet, $2\frac{1}{2}$ miles. From the summit, traverse N. on ridge to avoid the steep corrie slopes, and descend by obvious pinnacles down into the Stank Glen. Follow forestry road to Stank by Loch Lubnaig, $1\frac{1}{2}$ miles. St. Bride's Chapel is a short detour on the opposite side of the A84. From Stank, head N. by old railway line (first mile to holiday cottages on tarmac) which runs alongside the W. shore of Loch Lubnaig to Strathyre, 5 miles. Camp at campsite.

From the summit of Ben Lomond, looking roughly north-east, lies a fine land of loch, forest and mountain. It looks a wild area, though not as sterile and barren as other mountain areas of Scotland. These hills have a more intimate nature, their heights considerably less than their northern cousins; but what they lack in height, they more than make up for in character. Great corries biting into the hillsides, craggy bluffs and deep wooded ravines, and tumbling cascades of stone and scree showing where rushing streams have created fissures in the steep slopes. Long winding promontories, like great roots, flow down and disappear into the lapping waters of the lochs. Birch, oak, ash and pine decorate the shores and the lower slopes of the hills, and here and there, great grey upthrusts of rock burst from the foliage, like ancient craggy sentinels.

This is the area known as the Trossachs, a land celebrated in song and legend, and praised in pen by such notable worthies as Sir Walter Scott, the Wordsworths, and James Hogg. Indeed, it was the wonderfully descriptive pen of Sir Walter Scott who romanticized the Trossachs in *The Lady of the Lake*, and the Waverley novel *Rob Roy*.

> So wondrous wild the whole might seem,
> The scenery of a faery dream.

If the area was wild, its occupants in those far-off days were even wilder. The Trossachs region sits on the very edge of the Highland Line, a geological and geographical fault which runs across Scotland from the south end of Loch Lomond to Stonehaven on the north-east coast. The clans who inhabited the regions north of this line were, even until a comparatively late period, as Scott so succinctly puts it, "much addicted to predatory excursions upon their Lowland neighbours". Although the Trossachs were situated on the edge of this line, a border country almost, it was virtually sequestered from the world, and, as it were, insulated with respect by society. Graham's *Sketches of Scenery in Perthshire*, published in 1806, explains: " 'Tis well known, that in the highlands, it was in former times, accounted not only lawful, but honourable, among hostile tribes, to commit depredations on one another; and these habits of the age were perhaps strengthened in this district, by the circumstances which have been mentioned. It bordered on a country, the inhabitants of which, while they were richer, were less warlike than they, and widely differenced by language and manners."

The word "Trossachs" itself is derived from *Trosaichen*, a word now obsolete in the Gaelic language meaning a transverse glen joining two others. This description very loosely fits the heartland of the Trossachs area, the great tumble of rock and trees which separates Loch Katrine from Loch Achray. It was here that I parked my car after driving north from Glasgow one fine April morning. Loch Katrine is now a reservoir supplying water to the good citizens of the Glasgow metropolis, and a steamer, appropriately named *Sir Walter Scott*, plies the loch with daytrippers during the summer months. The season had not yet started though, and as I shouldered my pack and left the pier car-park, the place was deserted. It was a misty morning, with every promise of a great day ahead, and I could almost sense the sun trying to filter through the greyness above. Chaffinches and tits rollicked around on the branches of the trees which clothe the gorge, and a pheasant honked a morning greeting somewhere on the lower slopes of Ben Venue.

The road from the car-park runs for about a mile to its junction with the A821 Aberfoyle to Callander road, a particularly beautiful stretch of road through the wooded gorge which is formed between Ben Venue in the south, and rocky Ben A'an in the north. The green buds of the oak, larch and birch filtered the faint sunlight into a golden hue, and what beams did manage to pierce the mist were like pale green spotlights.

Ben A'an was my first destination, and I relished the thought of sitting up there on its rocky crest soaking up a view which is often considered to be one of the finest in southern Scotland. In front of me, Loch Achray stretched out, its far shore hidden in the mist. The Trossachs Hotel, a large, white baronial-style building, stood beside the road, and immediately in front of it, a signpost indicated the path which leads up through the oaks and birch to Ben A'an. This is not a high hill as mountains go, a mere 1520 feet above sea level, but it is a rocky spire of tremendous character and offers more in its 1520 feet than many hills of twice that height. Rock climbers often enjoy warm summer evenings on the perfect schistose rock, and ramblers can enjoy the grassy approaches to the wee summit. As I reached the top after twenty minutes or so of gentle exertion, I could feel the warmth of the morning sun on my head. Here, on top of Ben A'an, the mist was being rapidly burnt off around me. Ben Venue, across the gorge of the Trossachs, stood out against a deep blue sky, and the summit slopes of the Crianlarich and Arrochar hills to the west stood out like islands on a white ocean. The lochs below me were still in cloud, and I sat there and soaked up the morning warmth in a totally supercilious pose, indicating rightly or wrongly, little commiseration for those below me who were starting their day's chores in drab greyness.

Ben A'an, in actual fact, was not the original name of this hill. The old Gaelic name was Am Binnein, the Rocky Peak, but that was changed, like some other local names, to suit the poetic licence of Sir Walter Scott. Scott has had a considerable influence on the area, an area which he obviously knew fairly well, and he was directly responsible for this trip that I had just set out on. Ever since reading *The Lady of the Lake* and *Rob Roy*, I had become enthralled by the history of the Trossachs area, and in particular, in the doings of the Gregorach, the Clan MacGregor. My own clan, McNeish, is a sept of the MacGregor clan, or as they were collectively known, Clan Alpine. Their motto, "Royal is my Race", gives proof of their belief that they were descended from King Kenneth MacAlpine. Their erstwhile chief, Rob Roy MacGregor Campbell, like the area he ruled, owes much of his fame to Scott, who painted a rather colourful picture of this Scots Robin Hood. Rob Roy, nevertheless, is undoubtedly one of Scotland's best-loved heroes. He became chief of the MacGregors through sheer personality rather than by virtue of descent, and, although a rogue and scoundrel of the first order, he had a cheeky, albeit clever, manner, which endeared him to the common folk. My favourite tale concerning Rob is of an incident in the year 1716, when, on his way from

Inversnaid on Loch Lomondside to Aberfoyle, he was approached by a clansman with a sad tale to relate. A poor widow, a MacGregor, who was a tenant on the Duke of Montrose's estate, had fallen into arrears with her rent, and that very day, all her goods and chattels were to be sold by the Duke's factor to make up the debt. Rob, as ever concerned about the welfare of his clansfolk, called on the widow, advanced her the sum which was due, telling her that when the factor arrived, she was to give him the money, and make certain that she obtained a receipt for it. Not far from the widow's cottage, there was an inn at which the Duke's factor invariably stopped for refreshment whenever he was in the area. When he arrived, after collecting the money from the widow, he was confronted by the ominous bulk of Rob Roy and several of his ghillies, who, firmly yet politely, relieved him of all the money in his possession! Rob Roy was no longer out of pocket, and the widow had a receipt to prove that she had paid her annual rent. Such was the style of Rob Roy MacGregor.

Rob was born on 7th March 1671 in a little house at Glengyle, near to the head of Loch Katrine. He was baptized Robert, son of Lt-Col. Donald MacGregor, an officer in the army of Charles II, and Margaret Campbell, half-sister to the later despised Campbell of Glenlyon, who was responsible for carrying out the evil orders at the Massacre of Glencoe in 1692. As the name MacGregor was at that time proscribed, the local minister refused to carry out the baptism, and Donald had to carry the young Rob to the adjoining parish of Buchanan. This proscription of the name MacGregor occurred after a clan battle with the Colquhouns of Luss on Loch Lomondside. The MacGregors had always been a pretty volatile crew, but were in many ways no worse than other Highland clans. Feuding, stealing and cattle reiving had been a way of life in the Highlands for centuries, but in 1593, James IV of Scotland became determined to reduce the chaos of the Highlands to some sort of law and order, and he did not care whom he set as an example. James was responsible for bringing into effect an act known as the General Band, or Bond, which the Scottish parliament had passed as long ago as 1587 but had never really enforced. If any clansman was accused of a crime, his landlord must produce him to answer the charge, or pay the damages himself. The Act was designed to disrupt the clan system, and it certainly caused problems. The chiefs found themselves paying through the nose for the actions of their clansfolk. Alasdair of Glenstrae, the MacGregor chief at that time, eventually appeared himself before the court, and promised that his people would forthwith behave in a lawful manner and be answerable to King and Justice. This was a rather rash promise, and obviously Alasdair did not know his people as well as he thought, for despite his promise, the reivings and raidings inevitably went on.

Unfortunately, an incident occurred that brought matters to a head. Two MacGregors, on returning from a fair in Glasgow where they had been selling wares, stopped at a cottage in Luss for refreshment. The crofter, a Colquhoun, refused in no uncertain terms, a most unusual action since hospitality to travellers, even to one's enemies, was virtually sacrosanct in the Highlands. The two MacGregors, somewhat put out by this rebuff, decided to spend the night in a nearby barn, and, in lieu of what they felt was their rightful due, helped themselves to a sheep. Unfortunately, the MacGregors were either stupid or spiteful, or possibly both, for of all the sheep they could have taken, they killed the only animal in the flock with a black fleece and white tail. Needless to say, its loss was quickly spotted by the already suspicious Colquhouns; the MacGregors were quickly pursued, found with the sheep skin in their possession, and hanged on the spot. After this incident, Ian Dubh of Balquhidder, Alasdair of Glenstrae's brother, and one of the most volatile of the sept chieftains, took this incident as an excuse for revenge. The winter of 1601-2 had been a bitter one, harvests had been bad, and the unusually good behaviour of the MacGregors had simply resulted in a low larder. With Ian

Dubh biting his ear for action, and the clansfolk clamouring for revenge on the Colquhouns, Alasdair resignedly decided that he could not hold his people back. He might as well join them, and forthwith led an attack on Colquhoun lands. The first attack resulted in a hundred and twenty head of cattle being driven to MacGregor land. No one was killed. Six months later, a cousin of Alasdair's penetrated Glen Kinglas, in the heart of Colquhoun country, and ransacked it. Three hundred cows, four hundred sheep, and a hundred horses were driven out; cottages and barns were burnt to the ground, and two Colquhouns were killed. It is thought unlikely that Alasdair knew anything of the plans for this raid, but it marked the beginning of the end for the Clan MacGregor.

The Laird of Colquhoun, determined for revenge, decided to go and see King James himself, who was holding court in nearby Stirling Castle. Now, it was a well-known fact throughout Scotland that James could not stomach the sight of blood, so cunningly, the Laird of Colquhoun recruited some womenfolk from his clan to be passed as newly made widows. Carrying blood-stained shirts, most probably the blood of some purposely killed sheep, on the point of a spear, the women paraded into Stirling Castle, and barracked the king with loud wailings and sobbings. James was duly affected, and immediately granted Colquhoun Letters of Fire and Sword against the MacGregors. It has been recorded that the women returned home, getting themselves rollicking drunk in the process to celebrate their little act, and Colquhoun mustered an army of three hundred horse and five hundred foot to teach the Gregorach a final lesson.

Alasdair duly gathered his own men in self-defence, and joined up with Ian Dubh. They decided to take the initiative, and promptly marched to meet Colquhoun. The two forces met in Glen Fruin, a strategic advantage for the predominantly infantry forces of the MacGregors. The Colquhoun horse were next to useless in the bogland and deep heather of the glen, and the battle soon became a rout as Colquhouns fled in retreat. One hundred and twenty Colquhouns died. Unfortunately, the Battle of Glen Fruin further tainted the name of MacGregor rather than glorify it, as a large number of Colquhoun prisoners were stripped bare, and stabbed to death in cold blood. This evil deed was allegedly carried out by a MacDonald of Glencoe, one Alan Oig MacIntach, into whose care the prisoners had been put. MacIntach, a hired mercenary, committed his foul deed, possibly because of some personal vendetta against the Colquhouns. Whatever the reasons behind his actions, it was the MacGregors who were to carry the blame. Not that they were entirely blameless, however; every house, cottage and stack was burnt to the ground, everything which could be moved was carried off. The remaining Colquhouns were left with wailing womenfolk, screaming children, no roofs over their heads, no livestock and no crops. And all this in the bleak coldness of a January dawn! What the Colquhouns suffered was little though, in comparison to the evil events which were to befall the Gregorach.

Two days before King James left Scotland, in 1603, to take his place on the throne of England, an Act was passed, proclaiming that no man, woman, or child would be allowed to go by the name of MacGregor, on pain of death. Those MacGregors who took part in the Glen Fruin affair were branded as rebels, and entirely innocent MacGregors, the length and breadth of the country, had to change their name, usually at a high monetary cost. Worse was to come; anyone, according to this new law, was at liberty to kill a MacGregor on sight, and claim his goods and lands. Any known criminal or murderer would receive a pardon, if he could produce a MacGregor, dead or alive. The law applied to all the male members of the clan over the age of fourteen. The women were not forgotten though. The MacGregor womenfolk were to be branded on the face and transported, and their children, no matter what age, were to be left to fend for themselves.

This savagery and inhumanity shocked even hardened clan chiefs well used to cruelty and suffering. Many of the other clans, even erstwhile enemies like the Stuarts, were fined by the Government for helping MacGregors. The Gregorach took to the hills, hiding in caves and howffs. Stealing was the only course open to them. They slept by day and flitted like shadows into the glens at night to steal food for their families. These nocturnal doings soon earned them the name Children of the Mist.

As the years went on, things grew worse. The proscription had not worked. In time, all the MacGregors of consequence had either submitted to the Government, or had been killed. The clan was scattered far and wide, living totally outside the law, homeless; living on their wits, plundering, reiving; vagabonds and outlaws. The name MacGregor became one which struck fear and dread into the hearts of law-abiding citizens, whether Highlander or Lowlander. The Government retaliated. A free pardon was offered to any MacGregor who produced a MacGregor head of equal rank to his own. If the women betrayed their husbands, they were spared the brand. Death was pronounced on anyone who bore the name MacGregor, or wore the clan tartan, and on any MacGregor if he or she carried a weapon, other than a pointless knife for cutting meat.

This new-found notoriety was used to advantage by some of the smarter MacGregors. A blackmail business was set up. Bands of men protected the cattle of the rich merchants and farmers who lived on the borders of the Highland Line, in turn for an annual fee. In a short time, this protection racket became big business, and was even later approved by the Government, no doubt delighted to see the rebels settle down as prosperous business men, albeit shifty and unscrupulous ones. These Watches, as they were known, were set up throughout the Highlands, and Rob Roy's father became joint Captain of the Highland Watch. (The Watches were later turned into armed forces, hence the birth of the Black Watch Regiment.) Soon, the members of the various watches took a high social position in the clan set-up; they were in the privileged position of being allowed to carry arms, and they could exercise authority over their neighbours. This authority was often flouted, and a great amount of cattle stealing, or lifting, went on as well, under of course, the respectable and approved mask of the Highland Watch.

Rob's father, particularly infamous for his "lifting" exploits, died in 1693 so the responsibility of the clan chieftaincy, and the captaincy of the Highland Watch, fell on Rob's young shoulders. Rob was not actually in the line of descent for such titles, being only the second son, but such was his personality and influence over his elder brother John, even at the age of twenty-two, that his brother declined the responsibilities in favour of Rob.

Only a few weeks after Rob became clan chief, another Government ban was enacted on the Clan MacGregor, probably because it was felt that the clan was becoming too strong again. So Rob took the name Campbell, his mother's name, but more important the name of his cousin, the Earl of Breadalbane, who, in the future, was to become a strong benefactor when things didn't quite go Rob's way.

Rob Roy was not tall, but his broad stocky build, and strong personal charisma, stood him head and shoulders above others in almost any social gathering. It is said that nature endowed him with unusually long arms, so long that he could tie his garters below the knee without having to stoop. This "deformity" was put to much use when wielding a claymore, and for "lifting" other folk's cattle. He had a crop of fiery red hair, and a fine hair of the same shade covered his body, arms and legs. His eyes were of a penetrating blue, and he was born with a volatile nature to match his red hair. It is said that he could change from cold anger to uproarious laughter at the drop of a hat, and he had a devilish sense of humour, enjoying practical jokes, and, in particular, putting one over on authority. He had vowed to help the downtrodden, and in those wild days, protection like that meant a strong show of muscle and arms. He ran his Highland Watch in a shrewd business-like manner, and woe betide anyone who was late with his dues, whether he was the local minister, or the Lord Justice Clerk; Rob Roy was no great respector of persons.

The Trossachs area which now lay around me in the morning sunshine was MacGregor country, a rough and tumbled land which was used to advantage by the clan throughout the centuries. The route that I had come to follow was that course taken by the bearers of the Fiery Cross, or Crean Tarigh, the Cross of Shame; because disobedience to what the symbol implied, inferred infamy. When a chieftain desired to summon his clan, upon any sudden or important emergency, he slew a goat, and making a cross of any light wood, seared its ends in the fire, and then extinguished the flames in the blood of the slain animal. The symbol was then carried round the clan lands, and areas which owed allegiance to the patriarch of the clan, by a relay of runners, who passed the cross to each other with a single word, the place of rendezvous. At the sight of the Fiery Cross, every man, from age sixteen to sixty and capable of bearing arms was obliged to present himself instantly at the given rendezvous. He who failed to appear, suffered the extreme punishments of fire and sword, which were emblematically demonstrated to the disobedient by the bloody and burnt marks on the warlike cross. In Scott's "The Lady of the Lake", the cross was carried from "Lanric Mead", nowadays known as Lendrick, at the west end of Loch Vennachar, one of the lochs now shimmering below me. This was the traditional assembly point for the Gregorach, and it was near here, at Duncraggen, that "Angus, heir of Duncan's Line", was summoned to carry the first stage of the Fiery Cross. According to Scott, Angus sped quickly along the shores of Loch Vennachar to Coilantogle, where he ascended the broad ridge of Ben Ledi, and dropped down steeply to the Pass of Leny.

Loch Vennachar is not the most pleasant of the Trossachs lochs, the hills on its south shore being rather flat and uninspiring. I was also rather anxious to avoid as much road walking as possible, which can be purgatorial on the legs and feet, especially in hot weather, so I decided to skirt a little of the original Fiery Cross route, and take a short cut, although it was rougher country, over the actual summit of Ben Ledi. Below my rocky perch on Ben A'an, Loch Achray was now glinting blue and silver in the sun; it was time to stop daydreaming about history and move.

In a sense it was a pity that the weather was not sombre and grey, more in keeping with the dire deeds of the clan fortunes and misfortunes, but one does not experience perfect weather on the hills of Scotland very often, so the opportunity must be grasped with both hands, not to mention feet. I'm sure even the battling Rob Roy would have appreciated the pale green buds of the springtime trees, the last remnants of the morning mist flitting on the surface of the loch, and that unmistakable peace which is only to be found early in the morning.

As I made my way along the roadside towards Brig o' Turk, two roe deer, a buck and a roe, darted out in front of me and scampered up the opposite embankment into the trees. A buzzard mewed from somewhere high above, and a pair of mallards flew off in a flurry of spray down the loch. Loch Achray is small, only about $1\frac{1}{2}$ miles long by a third of a mile wide, but it has a splendid charm. A church, St Kessog's, sits alone on a promontory, with a backcloth which comprises the bulky Ben Venue as though rising sheer from the end of the loch, a fine position for worshippers to admire on their way to Sunday services. Loch Achray is joined to Loch Vennachar by the Black Water, a marshy river covered by birch and oak trees. This marshy ground is a well-known gathering place for whooper swans in winter time.

Rather than march on to Lendrick, which I had visited often enough when youth hostelling at the old Lendrick Youth Hostel (nowadays known as the Trossachs Youth Hostel as the S.Y.H.A. become more commercially minded), I turned off the main road at Brig o' Turk, to take the very minor road to Glen

Riverside brew and feet dip

Washing day

Inverlochy Castle and Ben Nevis

Sgurr Choinnich Beag and Sgurr Choinnich Mor

Below Sgurr Eilde Mor in the Mamores

The Devil's Ridge in the Mamores

In the Trossachs above Loch Katrine

Loch Achray and Ben Venue

Rob Roy's grave in Balquhidder churchyard

St Kessog's Church, the Trossachs kirk

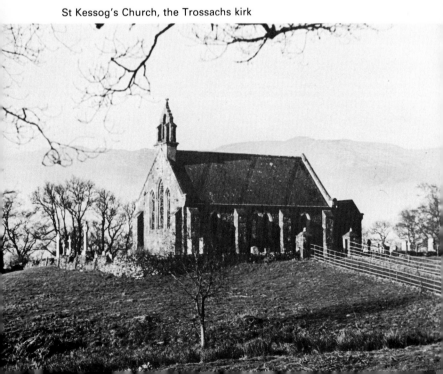

The bleak Mam na Cloich Airde

Loch an Dubh Lochain from Mam Barrisdale

Loch Hourn

Finglas Dam. Brig o' Turk is an odd-sounding name for a Highland village, and is derived from the Gaelic word *tuirc* meaning wild boar. Presumably these beasts were common hereabouts at some time in the past. In the days of Rob Roy, Brig o' Turk was a hamlet inhabited by wild drovers, and it had the reputation of being a pretty wild place. Today, it couldn't look tamer, the little cottages and well-kept gardens having a sleepy look about them. One or two faces peeped from behind closed curtains as I stomped past, no doubt wondering who could be disturbing their peace at such an early hour, and outside the tourist season too!

Glen Finglas, a fine glen between Ben A'an and Ben Ledi, is well and truly flooded by the waters of the Finglas Reservoir, part of the Strathclyde Regional Council Water Board system. Reservoir or not, apart from the dam at its head it does not look remotely artificial, and is as fine as any other Trossachs loch; even better than some. A bulldozed track runs from here to Balquhidder, a 10-mile walk through the Bealach a Chonnaidh, but this was not my route today. To the east rose the long broken and tufted slopes of Ben Ledi; the sun was warm, the sky blue, and I was eager to gain some height to enjoy the spectacle of a far-flung view. It is a good two miles to the summit of Ledi from Glen Finglas, with almost 2000 feet of climbing, but the going is easy over tufted grass and short heather. I had climbed Ledi often enough from the east, from Loch Lubnaig, but it is one of those hills of Scotland which tend to be largely ignored because they do not attain the magic 3000-foot Munro status. Nevertheless, it is an exciting hill with a good view, and some grand history attached to it as we will find out.

An old fence runs over the subsidiary top of Stuc Odhair, and down to the bealach which gives birth to Milton Glen Burn. On the opposite side of the bealach rise the final slopes of Ben Ledi. Rather than follow a direct line up the steep slopes to the summit, I traversed a little northwards, and climbed the gentler north-west ridge by way of some pleasant grassy gullies. As I reached the summit ridge, the white trig point which indicates the summit stood out like a beacon against the dark blue of the sky. The view was superb. All of the south, from the flats of Flanders Moss to as far as the eye could see, was covered by an ocean of cloud, with only the high tops of the Campsie Fells piercing the whiteness. Ben Lomond, the Beacon Hill, stood out as its name suggests it should, and to the north of it, the unmistakable outline of the Cobbler dominated the higher of the Arrochar Alps. All the Crianlarich and Glen Falloch hills could be easily identified, rising to the twin spires of Stob Binnein and Ben More. To the north-east, Ben Vorlich was hidden by its close neighbour, Stuc a Chroin, and beyond them, the great Lawers massif stood out clearly, white-fringed with snow against the blue. Below me, Loch Lubnaig and the Pass of Leny were barely discernible through a gossamer-thin film of mist, but the village of Callander was still submerged in cloud.

I made my way along to the trig point and cairn. The exact derivation of the name Ben Ledi seems to be unknown, the Gaelic name being Beinn Lididh; but the old *Statistical Account* suggests a possible derivation in the name Ben le Dia, the Hill of God. Flat stretches of turf on the summit ridge have been associated with the Beltane, or May Day Festival, which was held there annually. The ceremonies which took place were thought to be a version of a druidic ceremony which involved a human sacrifice to the Sun God Baal, the Baal of the Orientals; however, no stones or artefacts have been found to substantiate this theory. To heighten further the somewhat grisly aspect of the mountain's history, a small lochan lies about a mile north of the summit. This is Lochan nan Corp, or the small loch of the dead bodies. Centuries ago a cortège of mourners was following an old coffin route across the hill from Glen Finglas to St Bride's Chapel in the Pass of Leny, in the depths of winter. As they crossed the frozen waters of the lochan, the ice cracked open, and several of the mourners drowned in the bitter cold water below.

With the thought of frozen dead bodies, and human

sacrifices, I was glad that the sun was warm enough to take away the chill which was creeping up my spine. The summit of Ben Ledi, I decided, would be a place to avoid when on my own in misty weather. Not a place for a midwinter camp! To substantiate the feeling of mild apprehension, I noticed for the first time how evil the great eastern corrie of Ben Ledi looked. As I made the first few tentative steps down into the corrie, which leads down to the Stank Glen, the weird and fantastic jumble of rock outcrops and spires which decorate the slopes took on an almost malignant look; broken clawing shapes some fifty or so feet in height, towering above me like some malevolent crooked finger pointing out the road to Hades! The cirque of the corrie contains a forest of these formations, many of which would probably grace the halls of the Royal Academy, and although I had climbed amongst them often enough before, I had never thought of them as sinister. Perhaps it was because this was the first time I had climbed Ben Ledi knowing the history of its summit.

I had walked about 10 miles since leaving Loch Katrine, and with my daydreaming on top of Ben A'an, and the slow wander up Ben Ledi, it was now early afternoon. I had previously thought of bivvying in one of the rocky howffs below the rock outcrops, but it really was far too early. Besides I found myself rushing just a little through the rocks to reach the protection of the forest below! The village of Strathyre, with its pleasant little farm campsite, was another 8 miles on, including the short diversion to visit the remains of St Bride's Chapel, so I pressed on down through the forest trail of the Stank Glen. It was pleasant to walk in the shade for a while, and the pungent smell of the sun-warmed pine clung to my nostrils. I have always thought that the combination of pine and mountain air make a heady tonic, second only to the salt-scented combination of the west coast, the intermingling of sea and mountain air; marvellous for clearing a city head. The path was richly carpeted in pine needles, and it was a relief to walk on such a pleasant surface after the knee-jarring descent through the rocks and screes of Ben Ledi. I thought as I walked, how different it was for Sir Walter Scott's hero Angus as he fled down the hill with the dreadful symbol of war clutched firmly in his grasp. All indications in the poem show that the weather was probably foul; mention is made of mountain breezes, and to make matters worse, when he reached the foot of Ledi to hand the cross over to the next bearer, he found the River Teith in spate:

> Swoln was the stream, remote the bridge,
> But Angus paused not on the edge,
> Though the dark waves danced dizzily,
> Though reeled his sympathetic eye,
> He dashed amidst the torrents roar,
> His right hand the crosslet bore,
> His left the pole axe grasped to guide,
> And stay his footing on the tide.

My crossing wasn't anything so dramatic. I left my pack in the care of a kindly gentleman from Glasgow who had a holiday caravan at the foot of the glen. He had stopped me as I wandered past to offer me a cup of tea and a dram, in that order. It turned out that he was an old member of my old climbing club, the Lomond Mountaineering Club, long since retired from climbing, but enjoying the leisure of his retirement in this, one of his old wandering haunts. Strangely enough, he had never heard of the route of the Fiery Cross, so he locked my pack in his van, and came with me over the bridge to visit the ruins of the ancient chapel of St Bride. The ruins lie on the east bank of the River Teith, beside the busy A84 Callander to Lochearnhead road. Standing amidst the ruin and rubble it was hard to imagine bygone scenes. I related the story to my new-found companion. As Angus, dripping wet, staggered up the pathway to the church, a wedding was in progress. Unfortunately the next bearer in the relay of the cross was one Norman, heir of Armandave, who had just that minute got himself married to a young lass called Mary. As he escorted his blushing bride from the Gothic arch of the chapel, his thoughts were far from running alongside Loch Lubnaig with a cross in his fist.

> With virgin step, and bashful hand,
> She held the kerchief's snowy band,
> The gallant bridegroom by her side,
> Beheld his prize with Victor's pride,
> And the glad mother in her ear,
> Was closely whispering words of cheer,
> But, who meets them at the churchyard gate?

Who indeed? Brave Angus, sodden wet from his dook in the river and panting after his long run! And so poor Norman bade farewell for the time being to his new wife, and set off at a jog, cross in hand. My friend declared that he had never thought highly of Scott, much preferring the baser instincts of Rabbie Burns. Rabbie, no doubt, would have made more of the missed nuptials than Scott did! We retraced our steps to the caravan, and I lazed in the tiny little garden outside for a while, enjoying the crack and a large dram. I never did get the cup of tea!

From Stank, an old railway cutting hugs the western shore of Loch Lubnaig, and provides a first-class track for walkers. The busy road on the eastern bank of the loch should be avoided at all costs. It is always busy in the summer months, as it is the first Highland loch that northbound tourists come across on the road from Edinburgh. Because of this, the roadside is littered with viewpoints and laybys.

The first stretch of the old railway track has been asphalted, and my heart sank down to my bootlaces as I thought of 5 miles to Strathyre on a hard unforgiving road, especially as it was now hot in the mid-afternoon sun. My feet were to be spared though, as the hard surface only stretched for a mile or so to some Forestry Commission holiday cottages. Past the buildings, it became a rough track again, and I was happy enough to buckle down and enjoy the views up the loch through bushes of brilliant yellow broom. Some oystercatchers cried noisily overhead, and a pair of madcap lapwings cavorted crazily, diving and soaring in their deranged mating game.

The village of Strathyre, the "Bonnie Strathyre" of the song, is a tidy wee place at the head of Loch Lubnaig. At one time in the village's history it was known as Nineveh, because of the number of public houses it boasted. This was in the days of Rob Roy and Co., but nearby Balquhidder was even better, boasting no fewer than six public houses. They must have been a hard-drinking lot, the Gregorach. I camped in the pleasant little campsite just outside the village, in a little copse of oaks, and, in the name of research, felt obliged to sample at least one of the remaining pubs of Strathyre!

Cross the R. Balvag by the bridge just W. of the village, and almost immediately opposite, follow the forestry path signposted as Ben Shian. Follow this good track through forest, climbing to shoulder of hill S. of the summit. Leave the forest for the open hillside and begin descending, following marker posts, to Glen Buckie. Pass farm of Immerain (2 miles from Strathyre), cross the Calair Burn at Ballimore and follow minor road N.N.W. for $2\frac{1}{4}$ miles to Balquhidder. Slight diversion for churchyard and Rob Roy's grave. Follow the minor road, then track, on S. shore of Loch Voil, past Stronvar to Muirlaggan, $1\frac{1}{2}$ miles, where a bulldozed track strikes S.W. up the hillside. This track runs for $1\frac{1}{2}$ miles to a cottage just N. of the Bealach Driseach. Drop down to lochside beside the forest plantation, and follow faint track W., past Monachyle Tuarach, alongside the S. shore of Loch Doine to Blaircreich, S. of Inverlochlarig, 4 miles. Continue W.S.W. by river, and after $2\frac{1}{2}$ miles, contour around the north and west slopes of Stob a Choin, and climb slopes S. into high pass. Camp.

Continue S. by Allt a Choin to private road on N. shore of Loch Katrine, $2\frac{1}{2}$ miles, and follow this road E. for 8 miles to Trossachs Pier.

Directly west of the village, across the River Balvag, lies a long ridge of a hill called Beinn an t-Sithein, the Hill of the Fairies. Perhaps it is an indication of the unfortunate trend in anglicizing the old Gaelic names that the Forestry Commission have insisted in signposting the hill as Ben Shian, or that a hotel in Strathyre is called the Ben Sheann Hotel. I feel that this is an unfortunate trend and, in the long run, does not help visitors to understand the meaning of the Gaelic. The word *Sith*, meaning Fairy, is a word that hillwalkers and backpackers come across quite often in Scotland. The derivation *Shian* or *Sheann* tends to confuse one, and reduces the colourful, and often beautiful, Gaelic names to nondescript abbreviations.

My route lay across the ridge of this hill, over to the farm at Ballimore at the northern end of the Bealach a Chonnaidh, and then to Balquhidder, the final resting place of Rob Roy. The Forestry Commission, despite messing up the name of the hill, have proved their worth to us backpackers and hillwalkers by building a superb path up through their forest plantations on the eastern slopes of Beinn an t-Sithein. It is steep in places, but climbs quickly and gains height fast. I was astonished to find myself so high above Strathyre in such a short time as I left the trees and found myself on the broad heather-covered ridge. The morning had taken up where it had left off the night before; brilliant sunshine, and the night's frost had left cobwebs of silver patterns on the trees and heather. The track peters out shortly after leaving the forest, but a series of marker posts points the way down into Glen Buckie. To the north-west, the brown Braes o' Balquhidder, celebrated in Robert Tannahill's song of the same name, dominated the view, pockmarked here and there with tiny patches of white, the remnants of winter snow. To the west the mountains gradually grew higher until they almost choked together, a tumble of high craggy peaks, culminating in the high tops of the Crianlarich and Glen Falloch hills.

This second day of the Gregorach walk is an easy one after

the long 18 miles of the first day. The walk over Beinn an t-Sithein completes the climbing for the day; the rest of the day is a happy stravaig down to Balquhidder, then a lochside stroll up the glen beyond Inverlochlarig, a day of beautiful gentle scenery, plenty of history, with a tinge of sadness as we pass Rob Roy's last home at Inverlochlarig. From the farm at Ballimore, in Glen Buckie, a 2-mile stretch of road takes you downhill into the small village of Balquhidder. The latter third of this road stretch passes some delightful cottages. After the darkness of the forest, and the bareness of the open hill, this approach into Balquhidder is, in spring and summer, a myriad of colour, vibrant and dazzling. As you stroll round a bend in the roadway, your vision is suddenly blasted by the incredible profusion of colours. The broom and hawthorn were in bright flower, and the dazzling whitewash of the cottages made a glaring background to the brilliance of the gardens which were alive with azaleas and rhododendrons, bluebells, stitchwort and daffodils in bloom earlier than usual thanks to the mild winter of 1980-81, a symphony of colour which was as unexpected as it was beautiful. On the hillside opposite, pale young larches broke the monotony of dark green spruce, bringing the slopes to life. Balquhidder is not a large place, but it was near here that Rob Roy settled into married life, and it was here that he was eventually buried, in the tiny churchyard which has become a centre of attraction for visitors from all over the world.

My route turns off westwards before the Balvaig Bridge is crossed, passing Stronvar and Muirlaggan before following the south shore of Loch Voil and Loch Doine, but, although I have quietly visited the graveside of Rob Roy many times before, I felt that on this particular pilgrimage, the least I could do was pay my respects again to Rob and his family in the little churchyard. The kirk is an extremely picturesque one. Standing on a grassy knoll above the hamlet of Kirkton of Balquhidder, it offers a superb panorama of the Balquhidder glen. There are actually two churchyards; the original kirk, which dates from 1631, is now a ruin, and the new church stands behind it. The actual grave of the MacGregor chief is, in fact, unknown, but three monuments allegedly cover the final resting places of Rob, his wife Mary (called Helen by Scott) and two of their sons, Coll and Robin. The stones are typical late Scots medieval, there is no doubt about that, and the third stone certainly covers a MacGregor, as it displays the clan crest: a sword, a crown, and a pine tree which has been torn up by its roots. This uprooted pine symbolizes the tragic misfortunes of the proscribed clan.

Rob Roy's son, Robin, who rests here with his father, was mentioned in Robert Louis Stevenson's brilliant novel *Kidnapped*. He was known as Robin Oig MacGregor, and was reputedly a piper of the highest calibre. *Kidnapped*'s heroes, Alan Breck and David Balfour, were sheltering in a house belonging to a MacLaren, a traditional rival of the Gregorach. For some reason, Robin Oig calls, and is a little put out to find Alan Breck, a Stuart, there. Instead of fighting, it was suggested by the peaceable MacLaren that they have a piping contest, which the MacGregor won without too much difficulty. "Robin Oig," says Alan Breck in conceding victory, "ye are a great piper, I am not fit tae blaw in the same kingdom wi' ye. Body o'me, ye have mair music in yer sporran than I have in ma heid."

Returning to the south shore of Loch Voil, back across the triple arched Balvaig Bridge, I stopped for a moment to take in the view down the loch, one of the finest in the southern Highlands. Loch Voil has tiny wooded islands, promontories winding into the water, and on either bank, steep-sided hills, stretching back, fold upon fold, becoming paler and paler into the jumble of high mountains which fade into the far west.

I was a little concerned about the type of walking terrain I was to encounter on this stretch of lochside walking. I was using an old one inch to the mile scale map, and according to it, there was only a track as far as Muirlaggan, a third of the way along the lochside. This track passed the huge baronial-style building of Stronvar, which until six or seven years before had been a splendid youth hostel. Unfortunately, the upkeep of the place had become too much for the S.Y.H.A., and it was sold. It is now made into holiday flats. This stretch of shoreline is owned by Muirlaggan Estates, and, in addition to a caravan site at the east end of the loch, holiday caravans dot the shoreline. What impressed me very much was the obvious environmental concern of the Estate, for all these caravans were painted in subdued tones of green. Those who spend any time in the Scottish Highlands in summer will be aware of the problems which caravans cause, not only on the narrow roads, but through the visual offence they can cause when their bright colours and shiny metallic surrounds are seen from a distance, completely out of character with the predominant greens and browns of the countryside.

Just as the farm buildings of Muirlaggan came into view, a track, not marked on the one-inch map, breaks off uphill. It is signposted "Hikers This Way". After climbing for a couple of hundred feet, the track then runs parallel to the Muirlaggan one on the shoreline, and continues for another mile and a half. The track has obviously been bulldozed to service what appears to be a holiday cottage, a timber building, which, in the afternoon sun, looked Alpine in appearance. High above the spread of blue loch, the house and most of its garden were in the shade, all apart from one bright patch of daffodils which just caught the sun. I couldn't resist a photograph. What was intended as a brief photographic halt frittered into an ·hour's long laze. I brewed some tea, ate some oatcakes and cheese, and enjoyed one of the delights of backpacking: to linger when one feels like it, untied to timetables or hotel mealtimes. I lay on the heather beside the track and watched a buzzard circle on the thermals high above me. A lark sang briskly, one of my favourite bird songs, so full of the joys of life; a marvellous sound. The track ended here, and I had to decide whether to maintain height and try and find a way through the young forestry plantation, or drop down and chance my luck with the shoreline. I dropped down to the loch; down steepish heathery slopes, and joy of joys, immediately came upon a faint track running between the trees and the shingly shore. It was a little wet and boggy in places, and on several occasions I had to clamber over fallen branches, but it was far preferable to negotiating the deep furrows and prickly pines of the young plantation higher up the hill.

Loch Voil and Loch Doine are virtually one loch. Only a narrow spit of land and a short stretch of slow-moving river separate the two. In his book *The Scottish Lochs* Tom Weir explains that the separation of the two lochs is due to a build up of alluvium from the Monachyle Burn in the north, and the Monachyle Tuarach in the south, working towards each other. The farmhouse at Monachyle Tuarach was Rob Roy's first steading. Rob received the tenancy as a gift from his father in 1692. "Tuarach" means facing northwards, and because of this position, the farm could not receive a great amount of the day's sun. On top of this the flat lands around the building were liable to flood at the first hint of heavy rain, so arable farming was out of the question. Rob decided to concentrate on sheep farming, and soon became a well-known figure at the markets and trysts throughout Scotland. It was to this bachelor pad that Rob brought his young wife, Mary MacGregor of Comar, a distant cousin.

My visualizing of Rob Roy as a young farmer at Monachyle Tuarach was well and truly shattered when I actually reached the house. On the flats between the buildings and the lochside, three brightly painted wigwams, Red Indian tepees, were pitched, as out of place as haggis and champit tatties in a Manhattan restaurant! They belonged to an American/ Canadian group of youngsters who intended staying for the summer, trying, I imagine, to live like prairie indians. A far cry from the buffalo-haunted plains of the mid-west.

The track continued alongside Loch Doine, and I watched several pairs of mallards swimming in the tiny bays. Across the loch, the long craggy slopes of Stob Binnien and Beinn Tuleachean rose high, two Munros which I had climbed years before from Crianlarich, on the other side of the range. At the head of the loch stands the farm of Inverlochlarig, on the site of the house in which Rob Roy died on 27th December 1734. It was a peaceful death, so uncharacteristic after a life of daring, adventure and turmoil. The story of his last hours on earth have passed into legend. As he lay on his death-bed, he was informed by his ghillie that a MacLaren had come to pay his respects. Not wanting to be seen by an erstwhile enemy in his bedclothes, he commanded his assembled family to dress him in his plaid, and gather his weapons around him. He thus greeted his visitor. When the MacLaren left, Rob lifted himself up on his elbows and asked his piper to play the lament "Cha till mi Tuiidh", "I Shall Return No More". Before the piper had finished the dirge, Rob had passed away. His body was carried in great ceremony and mourning to Balquhidder, where he was buried and still lies today.

Leaving Inverlochlarig, I began the last stretch of the pilgrimage of the Fiery Cross; back through the hills to Loch Katrineside. It was now late afternoon, so I decided to head through the high pass of the Glen of Weeping, which skirts the western slopes of Stob a'Choin. The drooping sun was casting long shadows on the surrounding hills and a curlew gurgled in the distance. I almost expected to hear a lonely pibroch drift in the air up from the glen, but only the sound of the curlew broke the stillness; a sound comparable in sadness and expressiveness. I camped on the 1000-foot contour, beside a small lochan, and lay in the tent doorway to watch the sky turn orange, crimson, and then violet, before the glimmer of the first star heralded darkness. This second day had given me another 18 or so miles, with a small proportion of it on road.

I woke early to a thin drizzle; so much for the old saying: "A red sky at night is a shepherd's delight"! The shepherds hereabouts must be fishermen, the only people I know who appreciate a morning like this. Two stags were grazing contentedly about a hundred yards away, my green tent making them oblivious to my presence. They didn't look my way once, until my petrol stove roared into action and sent them bounding up the opposite slope. After breakfast and packing up, the weather began to clear a little, and a watery sun tried to ooze from a leaden sky. I made my way over boggy ground by the Allt a Choin, a meandering hill stream which flowed southwards into Loch Katrine. The final 10 miles were on the private road along the north shore of Loch Katrine. I had almost wished for a dark misty morning when I set out on this ploy, and now that wish had come true for my return. To the south-east, the riven bumps and bluffs of Ben Venue had a swirling layer of cloud and mist. The sky was broken in patches, glimpses of blue alternating with towering grey clouds, much more typical of Trossachs weather than the brilliance of the past two days.

The waters of Loch Katrine have been harnessed to supply the water needs of the city of Glasgow, but apart from the odd signpost telling you not to swim in the reservoir, all is unspoilt and natural until the eastern end of the loch, where the pier, the steamer, and the car-park stamps the marks of officialdom. Loch Katrine is possibly the most beautiful of the Trossachs lochs, and as usual, Sir Walter Scott summed it up succinctly in only four lines:

> High in the south huge Ben Venue,
> Down on the lake in masses threw,
> Crags, knolls, and mounds, confusedly hurled,
> The fragments of an earlier world.

Despite the false tidiness of the eastern shore, the bays and spits barriered by concrete embankments and iron railings, the view across the loch to Ellen's Isle and Ben Venue is still wild and wondrous. An ancient pass slices through the hillside of Venue between the summit and the loch, the Bealach nan Bo, where the Gregorach reivers drove their stolen cattle *en route* to Glengyle at the head of Loch Katrine. Below the bealach is a corrie called Coire nan Uruisgean, or Corrie of the Urisks, or Goblins. This was reputedly the meeting place for all the goblins in Scotland, who gathered here to plan and plot amid the deep heather and boulder-scarred hollows. These Urisks, explains Dr Graham in *Scenery of the Southern Confines of Perthshire*, published in 1806, "were a sort of lubbery supernatural, who could be gained over by kind attention to perform the drudgery of a farm. They were supposed to be spread throughout the Highlands each in his own wild recess, but the solemn meetings of the order were regularly held in this cave of Benvenew."

I wondered if there were any goblins in the corrie of Ben Ledi. As I approached the pier, and the end of my walk, it became apparent from the number of people I met that I was back in daytripperland. I had completely forgotten that this was Easter Friday. Despite the glowering weather, there were dozens of people about, parking their cars in the car park at the pier and walking a few dozen yards down the lochside before scampering back again. It struck me for the thousandth time that we backpackers have it all our own way. By actually getting into the countryside, away from the roads and towns, we can really submerge ourselves into the history and beauty of a place, completely and thoroughly. These poor daytrippers were scratching at the edges of what the Trossachs have to offer. Even if they knew of the work of Sir Walter Scott, or the doings of Rob Roy, they would go home from here little richer for the experience. I reached my car, put my pack in the boot, and bade farewell for the time being to the Trossachs, after three truly memorable days following in the footsteps of the

Children of the Mist. I felt richer for the experience, and felt something of the urge which prompted Scott into writing his splendid works.

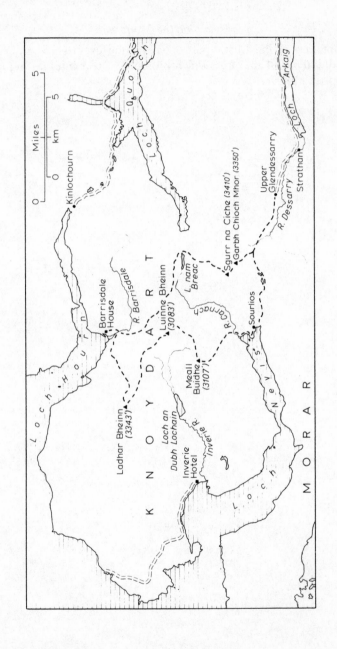

ROUTE 5: THE KNOYDART MUNROS

About 38 miles. A three-camp journey through some very difficult and remote terrain. Ascends 5 Munros. Not for the inexperienced.

Map required: O.S. 1:50,000 Second Series. Sheet 33.

From Strathan at head of Loch Arkaig walk N.W. on track past Glendessarry House, and Upper Glendessarry, 2 miles. Continue on track, over watershed and W. into Mam na Cloich Airde, passing Loch a'Mhaim. Follow path through pass and drop down long slopes to Sourlies, 6 miles. Follow coast of Loch Nevis N.W. and N. to Carnoch, 1 mile. Camp. Cross River Carnach (new bridge) and take the zigzag path which runs N.W. from the old ruins at Carnoch, up and into the Mam Meadail, 1½ miles. From high point of pass, ascend slopes of Meall Buidhe N. through crags to summit, 3107 feet. Follow ridge E. than N.E. around rim of Corrie Odhair to Luinne Bheinn, 3083 feet, 3 miles. Descend N.W. ridge to Mam Barrisdale and camp on high point of pass, 1¼ miles.

The spring rain was falling in cascades from dense grey cloud, and countless new waterfalls had been formed overnight on the slopes on either side of me. "Go to Knoydart in the spring," I had been told. "You can be fairly certain of settled weather then." The weather had been foul all the way over from Speyside and along the narrow road on the north side of Loch Arkaig the visibility had grown less and less. The close-set beech-tree stretch of road at the eastern end of the loch, the Mile Dorcha, or the Dark Mile, was well named today, and it was with a little trepidation that I locked up the car at Strathan, heaved my laden pack on to my shoulders, and set off westwards towards the Rough Bounds of Knoydart.

The Knoydart Munros: Meall Buidhe, Luinne Bheinn, Ladhar Bheinn, and Sgurr na Ciche, had been staring at me from my book of Munros Tables for an annoyingly long time. Their names lay there, unticked, aloof, and vaguely intimidating. All four are capable of being climbed on separate days, Ladhar Bheinn from Barrisdale on Loch Hournside, or from Inverie on Loch Nevis, and the other three from either Inverie, or Upper Glendessarry but such is the remoteness of the Knoydart area, that long approaches are necessary to reach any of the four Munros.

It seemed a good idea, seated beside the comfortable flicker and warmth of a winter's fire, to explore all four in one single backpacking expedition; stravaiging these far-flung western hills in total self-sufficiency, and untrammelled by the urgency of boat timetables or daylight hours. I had given myself four complete days, with three nights' camping, so my pack was fairly well stuffed with food and camping gear. There are no shops in this wild empty corner, in fact areas of habitation are negligible; the nearest being at Inverie on Loch Nevis, some six miles off my intended route.

I walked alone in Knoydart, not this time out of choice, but because I couldn't find a companion who could spare the free time to fit in with my own schedules. I had been anxious to share the trip with someone, purely for safety's sake, as this area, with the possible exception of the Great Wilderness between Loch Maree and Little Loch Broom, is about the most rugged in Scotland; hence its old title, the Rough Bounds of Knoydart. Seton Gordon, that marvellous old walker and naturalist, in his book *Highways and Byways in the West Highlands*, had described it thus: "A wild country of dark sea lochs and gloomy hills, often mist shrouded. Here the clans of the *uruisgean* or spectres must roam, here the *each uisge* and the *tarbh uisge*, the water bulls, perhaps fight fierce battles. I do not think the *daoine sith*, the hill faeries, are here. The country is too vast and forbidding for the little people."

Bill Murray, though, in the *Companion Guide to the West*

Highlands of Scotland, was a little more comforting and threw some sunshine on my plans: "These numerous glens and tracks, free from all motor traffic, give excellent walking through wild country ... They breathe a peace that other areas lack, they have a remoteness without desolation, and a beauty without blemish." Good, I was prepared to meet even the old *tarbh uisge* for the joy of walking in such an area.

Access to our hills must remain sacrosanct, and there is an undoubted challenge in obstacles and difficulties, provided that they are natural and not insurmountable. Challenge and difficulty there certainly is in Knoydart, but it is these aspects of the land which made Knoydart so attractive. Roads are non-existent, but paths and rights of way are good. I intended using them to the full.

And so I set out; I did not know whether I was more fearful or more looking forward to what was to come. Although it was wet, there was little wind and it wasn't cold, so I huddled up in my cocoon of waterproofs, rather uncomfortable but well protected in the micro environment, and began the 7-mile trek to Loch Nevis, where I could camp for the night somewhere in the vicinity of the bothy at Sourlies.

The track was a good one, shown as a road on Roy's Map of 1755. On the six-inch-to-the-mile map of 1876, it was marked as a second-class road. Today, it is one of a vast network of rights of way, so carefully documented by the Scottish Rights of Way Society Ltd, a watchdog organization that every walker who comes to Scotland should be thankful for. After 2 miles of easy walking in a north-west direction, I crossed the summit of the path at around a thousand feet above sea level, and made my squelchy way due west, through the Mam na Cloich Airde, the Pass of the High Rock, seeing very little beyond the waters of Lochan a'Mhaim and the streaming hillsides which seemed to grow wilder, rockier and more precipitous as I began the long descent to Loch Nevis. The gentle greenery of Glendessary was behind me now, and I had crossed the threshold into another world, a wilder more remote landscape. It was a sudden and spectacular change of environment. The path zigged and zagged in fine curves, crossing brown peat-stained streams, one in particular, the Allt Coire na Ciche, wider and requiring more care than the rest. This normally insignificant stream can double and even treble in size in a few hours of rain, and was the scene of a fatality earlier in the year when Donald Mill, an experienced and strong walker, was swept away and drowned whilst attempting to cross. A rope hung across the stream today. Was it an aid to crossing the roaring waters, or possibly a lure to the inexperienced? It seems to me that more people get into difficulties on rivers which have ropes hung across them than on those which don't. The false aid of a rope simply lures people into crossing where common sense would say stop, wait, or cross the river higher up where it is narrower. Too many people underestimate the strength of an in-spate Highland stream.

Once safely across the Allt Coire na Ciche, the narrow glen widens out to greet the shingly flats at the head of Loch Nevis. Several old buildings huddle together in this wild corner; one of them, Sourlies, has been renovated by the Mountain Bothies Association, and offers a dry shelter. I didn't succumb to the temptation of settling in for the night though, as one's movements hereabouts tend to be dictated by the state of the tide in Loch Nevis. As I arrived, the tide was just coming in, which meant that I could follow the barely discernible path which runs across the shingle beach between the tide lines. If the tide is high, you are faced with a rough scramble; the crags at the foot of the south-western ridge of Sgurr na Ciche fall steeply to the sea. I worked my way round the crags and pitched the tent on a green sward riven on all sides by little channels. It was a good spot. Despite the greyness of the weather, the rain had stopped, and one or two brighter areas beamed their way on to the surface of the loch. All around me came the cry of gulls, the loon-like cry of the herring gull in particular, an exulting kaaaa-reeee, which, in the half light and half dark of the gloaming, evoked in me a strange feeling. It was the sound of mindless wastes of water, the cry of a soul which is not a soul; weird, lost, doomed, and yet, strangely, totally triumphant. A cry of invincible wildness!

The first obstacle encountered in the morning was the swift-flowing River Carnach. I had been warned that people had drowned here trying to cross when the river was in spate, and that the best place to cross was at the estuary at low tide. At the time of my visit, the bridge which is marked on the O.S. 1:50,000 map did not exist, but as I write, a group from St Andrews University and the Mountain Bothies Association are rebuilding it, amid much controversy. Many people believe that wild areas like Knoydart should be left as they are, both as a tonic, and a challenge. To build bridges is an intrusion which tries to tame and demean the hills, a game which is both immoral and unfair. Wilderness areas are few, wilderness being an absence of all intrusive human objects, and if someone wishes to walk in such an area then surely that person must be competent and fit to do so, and that includes learning to cross rivers, or, as the case may be, knowing when not to attempt to cross a river. Do climbers try and tame a difficult cliff face by putting in a ladder? Of course they don't, they accept the risk of the climb and so enjoy it all the more. It's a pity that many authorities don't yet realize that many walkers and backpackers also seek and relish a risk factor. In my opinion, the building of a new bridge over the Carnach will only encourage inexperienced walkers into an area which has as many potential dangers as the often quiet River Carnach. Will they build bridges over all the rivers in Knoydart?

The tide was on the ebb again, and I managed to wade across at the river's mouth, boot laces tied together and slung around my neck. I have never found river wading to be particularly pleasant, never mind first thing in the morning, but I managed to reach the west bank with nothing worse to show than a pair of blue feet. I dried my feet off as best as I could, and wandered up past the keeper's old cottage at Carnoch, sadly now no more than a shell. Ben Aden's great whaleback loomed through the drizzle which persisted desultorily, as though someone had forgotten to switch it off. My route was now via the hill pass of Mam Meadail which runs roughly westwards from Carnoch to Inverie. An excellent track, with a series of tight hairpin bends, winds its way through some rough ground, climbing into the pass. As I climbed, I took the odd look behind me, hoping for a glimpse of Sgurr na Ciche, but only a momentary glimpse, as its sharp head appeared through a hole in the cloud, gave me promise of its real majesty. Sgurr na Ciche is a striking mountain, one of the most impressive in the west, especially when seen from Loch Nevis, and I was looking forward to getting to grips with it. But that was two days in the future.

I stopped just over the summit of Mam Meadail, at 1700 feet, with Inverie Bay glinting steel grey below me. This was where I had to decide whether the weather was going to turn me back or not. I had two mountains to traverse in the course of the day, Meall Buidhe and Luinne Bheinn (known to crazy Munro-baggers as Loony Bin), in the course of the day, a traverse which would take me into the very heart of the Rough Bounds of Knoydart. Once committed, it would mean a long long walk back to Glendessary again, crossing high passes and some of the roughest terrain in the country. I took stock; the weather was, for the moment anyway, pretty bleak, but not terribly bad. To one used to backpacking in Scotland rain was an occupational hazard which had to be endured. If it wasn't, there would be little point in taking up backpacking in the first place; you would very rarely go out! I was fit, well stocked with food, had a dry sleeping-bag and a tent, and was competent enough in finding my way around. To turn back would be an admission of defeat which was unthinkable in my dry, fresh state. Convinced, I turned due north, and began climbing a gully which eventually spewed me out on top of the south-east shoulder of Meall Buidhe, the Yellow Lump. The dark green eye of Loch Nevis glinted below, Ben Aden now showed more clearly through the thin mists, rather than just a big dark lump, and joy of joys, there was the spiky cap of Sgurr na Ciche, clear of cloud at last and dominating everything around it. A short pull up, my only effort at navigation being that I kept on an upwards line, through some crags, and I was on the summit ridge. I followed the rim of the cliffs which fall away to the north into Choire Odhair, and soon reached the grassy summit. I was in cloud again, so was cruelly denied the view down Loch Nevis, the Loch of Heaven, that I had hoped for. However, the view across Choire Odhair to the north, where my next stop, Luinne Bheinn, lay, more than made up for it. The steep slopes of Meall Buidhe lay like embossed armour plating, the steep slabs running and glistening with running water. Below Luinne Bheinn, innumerable tiny lochans were caught in footholds in the precipices, and the slopes to the summit looked forbiddingly steep. Cramming some chocolate into my mouth, I began slowly descending the steep north-eastern ridge of Buidhe; a long steep bumpy ridge, with good drops on either side. Reaching the north-east arm of Luinne Bheinn, I worked my way up, through and over some craggy ground to gain the eastern top, where a short easy walk took me on to the real summit, 3083 feet above Loch Hourn far below. I gazed down at the depths in which this great loch lay, surrounded by high steep mountains, ghostly in the nebulous light created by the soft wet haze. This loch has been described as the grandest of the fissures which tear Scotland's west coast; reaching far and deep inland from the Sound of Sleat to the roadless forests of Glenelg and Knoydart, it winds tortuously into the heart of the country, more like a great Norwegian fjord. Seton Gordon compares it to a lake of the infernal regions, and the comparison is not at all fanciful; indeed, there is an aura of mystique which Loch Hourn has acquired through Gaelic mythology as the ancestral home of *Domhnull Dubh*, the Devil. Hourn is a corruption of *Iutharn* which means Hell!

Meall Buidhe and Luinne Bheinn, curiously, must be in some

form of mountain limbo, perched precariously between Heaven and Hell! Loch Nevis, the Loch of Heaven, is fairly open and usually pleasant, while Loch Hourn is normally in the sun's shade, even in summer. Perhaps it's an indication of my eventual destination, in that of the two, I definitely prefer Loch Hourn, for all its darkness. Its whole character is more appealing, more dramatic than Nevis, grand, mysterious. I had a sudden notion of canoeing its length some time.

To the north-west, the steep crags and bluffs of Ladhar Bheinn (Larven) were clear of cloud, my hill of the morrow. Down the steep north-north-west ridge of Luinne Bheinn I went, the bonnie valleys that run up from Barrisdale Bay half revealing themselves, down to the summit of the track which runs from Inverie to Barrisdale to Loch Hournside. It was now late afternoon, and I camped beside the track, not far from a spring of cold, clear water. As I put the tent up, a watery sun finally managed to break the monopoly of cloud, and oozed its beams earthwards. Even the slight light it emitted enhanced that grim environment, and brought glistening colours to what, all day, had virtually seemed like a monochrome landscape. The rain had finally been turned off, and a cool breeze brought with it the tangy scent of the sea. The combination of salt tang and pure mountain air is a heady tonic to which one can easily become addicted. The Scottish west coast blend is particularly evocative, a scent which reminds me of marvellous past days which I associate with the West of Scotland. Others have mentioned the same experience.

Climb long shoulder of Ladhar Bheinn to N. and E. of Coire a'Phuill and follow ridge of Ladhar Bheinn to summit, 3343 feet, $2\frac{1}{2}$ miles. Descend to Barrisdale Bay by way of the Druim a'Choire Odhair, $2\frac{3}{4}$ miles. Walk S. past cottage of Ambraigh and take path S. and S.E. into Gleann Unndalain. Climb slopes through glen to Lochan nam Bhreac, 5 miles. Camp. Continue on path E.S.E. to head of Loch Quoich, walk S. and after $\frac{1}{2}$ mile strike W.S.W. up steep slopes of Meall a Choire Dhuibh. Follow ridge to Sgurr na Ciche, 3410 feet, 4 miles. Descend S.E. to bealach and climb to summit of Garbh Chioch Mhor, 3350 feet (newly promoted Munro). Follow obvious ridge E. for $\frac{3}{4}$ mile and descend long slopes to Mam na Chloich Airde track, $2\frac{1}{2}$ miles. Return to Strathan by Glendessarry, $4\frac{1}{2}$ miles.

I woke up at 8 a.m., stiff and sore from a night sleeping on lumps and bumps of tussocky grass which had seemed perfectly comfortable the night before. North-west and west of me, the steep slopes of Ladhar Bheinn, the Forked Mountain, rose dramatically. The normal approaches to this hill are on the south-west side of the mountain from Folach in Gleann na Guiserein, or from Coire Dhorcaill, the great howked-out corrie which bites into the mountain from the north-east. I intended descending into Coire Dhorcaill from the summit, a route which would take me down to Barrisdale Bay on Loch Hourn, so I simply grabbed my pack, buckled down, and attacked the slopes immediately in front of me. The sun was putting in a fair effort to burst from a cloudy sky, a sky which looked as though it would clear with a whiff of wind, and I felt good. I took a "come what may" attitude, theoretically a bad attitude to take in the hills, but one which, this morning, proved to be quite effective. A long slow pull on grassy slopes took me to the first steep shoulder above Coire a'Phuill; a long green gully to the left bypassed the crags, some of which looked vertical; and a little scrambling soon had me on the ridge north-east of Aonach Sgoilte. Once up here, the long magnificent hugeness of Ladhar Bheinn rose, fell, then rose again. In front of me to the right, were the great depths of Coire Dhorcaill, to the left the long grassy slopes of Coire Torr an Asgaill. I traversed the bumps and dips on the ridge, some of the descents being a bit on the rough side, with a little rock scrambling in places, but with even more rock dodging. The final ridge was narrow and exciting, but never knife-edged, the left-hand slope being at a comfortable angle, and it didn't take long before I stood on the first of the mountain's tree tops. These tops are all around the same height, all linked by an easy walk to the main summit at 3343 feet. I walked on to the trig point on the westerly summit, hoping against hope that a few extra yards west would improve the view, but no such luck. Distant views were well and truly obscured by a thin haze, which was a pity, as Ladhar Bheinn, being the most westerly Munro on the mainland, offers a seascape second to none. Or so I am told! A tiny boat pulsed down Loch Hourn far below me, the only sign of civilization that I could see. It had taken me almost two hours to clamber up the hill, and it was not yet noon. Plenty of time to enjoy it. From the summit, a knobbly ridge leads in a north-easterly direction to a subsidiary top, Stob a Choire Odhair, and from there, another ridge, the Druim a'Choire Odhair, unwinds in a wide sweep eastwards, and then east south-east, down to rough grassy slopes which form the skirts of Coire Dhorcaill. On the south-east side of the stream which issues from the corrie, a stalkers' track zigzags its rough way down to the flats which surround Barrisdale Bay.

I lay at ease beside the stream and took in the surroundings. Old Barrisdale House is now a farm, and sheep and several cows grazed quietly on the rich green flats above the high-tide mark. The waters of Loch Hourn are more benign here than anywhere else in its whole length; the white shores clean and bright, and the small islands emerald green. It was a peaceful scene, but times weren't always so quiet.

The Barrisdale Macdonnells were "out" with Dundee at the Battle of Killiecrankie, and later fought under the banner of Glengarry at the Battle of Sheriffmuir during the first of the Jacobite rebellions. Coll, or Colla, Ban, so named because of his fair complexion, was perhaps the most celebrated of the Barrisdale Macdonnells. He was captain of the Highland Watch on the west side of Inverness-shire, a highly respected and important position. At the Raising of the Standard at

Glenfinnan in 1745, Coll Ban marched at the head of the Knoydart Macdonnells to join up with the forces of Charles Edward Stuart, the Young Pretender. He so distinguished himself at the Battle of Prestonpans that he was made a Knight Baronet, but, unfortunately, was captured at the ill-fated rout of Culloden. He escaped execution on the condition that he supplied information as to the whereabouts of the Bonnie Prince. Telling the Duke of Cumberland that the Prince was in hiding with some Campbell friends in Perthshire, he secured his release. The Prince was in fact at that time skulking in the Hebrides, and it seems strange that Cumberland, an astute commander, was taken in by Coll's story. When the information proved false, a party of Rosshire militia was sent to Knoydart to find Coll, and burn down Barrisdale House. Coll once again escaped, this time to France aboard a French man-of-war, but the Prince, believing that Coll had indeed plotted against him, made him a prisoner. Once again he escaped, only to be imprisoned again on his return to Britain. He died in captivity in Edinburgh, very possibly a victim of great injustice.

After the '45, a long-drawn-out period of emigration from Knoydart began. A combination of potato blights and the failure of the migrating herring shoals to arrive in anything like their old numbers brought famine and dire poverty to the area. The chief at the time, Aeneas of Glengarry, sold all his lands except Knoydart, and sailed to Australia, only to return in 1852, to die at Inverie. After his death, his widow, Josephine Macdonnell, began to make for herself one of the most hated and foul reputations in the annals of the history of the clearances, viciously clearing the remaining tenants to make way for sheep. Four hundred people were evicted by the most evil methods, their homes being burnt around them, and hounded like animals on to awaiting transport ships supplied by the British Government.

No cailleach's scream, no bodach's dream, can overcome the fate,
To live the life, to know the strife, of destitutes of hate.
As I gaze o'er that lonely shore, my heart breaks and I weep,
Those noble people, so proud, so simple, being cleared away,

                                                    for sheep.

Aye, it's a sad history, a history that even today leaves its mark on the atmosphere of this and other places, scattered throughout the western seaboard of Scotland. I mooched around for a while, enjoying the sunshine that tried to penetrate the dark fastness of the loch, ate a large lunch of oatcakes, cheese and German sausage, an unlikely combination, but containing enough gut stickability to keep me going for the rest of the afternoon. Breathing enough garlic to keep all the vampires of Hades at bay, I moved off southwards again, to where the Mam Barrisdale track began wriggling its way up the steep slopes. Past the ruined cottage at Ambraigh, I left the Mam track, and followed another, southwards, and then south-westwards, into Gleann Unndalain. This is another of Knoydart's rights of way, through a beautiful glen which crosses to the head of Loch Quoich below the northern flanks of Luinne Bheinn and Ben Aden. I crawled up the path to the summit of the glen, at over 2000 feet, a long pull which made me feel weary and heavy despite my long linger at Barrisdale. A huge herd of red deer were browsing in the bealach, and I felt the ground actually shake as they careered off, south-westwards.

The topmost towers of Ladhar Bheinn were glowing in the sun behind me, and the steep craggy slopes of Luinne Bheinn rose protectingly above me. I had the strong enveloping sensation that the Rough Bounds of Knoydart were all mine, that I had earned the peace, the solitude and the unspoilt beauty of the place. With this satisfying glow, the tiredness seemed to flow from my legs, and I wandered happily down the glen to Lochan nam Bhreac, a wild and lonely lochan as atmospherically perfect as any. The approaches to this loch wind through and over precipitous moraines and mounds which fall down to the stream in the cradle of the pass. In front, the long arm of Loch Quoich stretched eastwards, its surface actually higher than Lochan nam Bhreac's. I cut down from the path before it descended to the eastern end of the lochan, and found a small sandy bay fringed by a flat stretch of turf; an ideal campsite. I had looked forward to a bathe all afternoon whilst struggling up and through the pass, but now, as the bitter cold water reached above my thighs, I made do with a rough and ready wash before clambering ashore goose-pimpled and blue. A largish supper of soup, curry, and freeze-dried strawberries soon warmed me up, and I dozed off to the sound of thrumming snipe. Knoydart had been kind to me, and I could hardly believe my good fortune. I went off to bed hoping my luck would hold out for another day.

Sgurr na Ciche and home was the new itinerary. The morning looked promising enough, and I breakfasted and packed to the rhythm of a bleedin' bleeping plover which had begun at five and bleeped on and on like a blasted cuckoo. Some birdsong is a joy to wake up to, like the gurgling of a curlew, or the yelping hoot of a lapwing, but cuckoos and plovers are monotonous songsters, at least at five o'clock in the morning they are. I forded the shallow end of the lochan, and followed the track west-south-west, between the slopes of Ben Aden and a humpy hillock on the left. A red deer hind stood on top watching me warily. At the head of Loch Quoich, the track forks, one branch to where Kinlochquoich Lodge used to be before the valley was flooded by the Hydro-electric Board, and the other branch turning right towards Coire nan Gall on the eastern slopes of Sgurr na Ciche. I passed the small dam, and followed the old stalkers' path south, then, after half a mile or so, westwards up the hillside. The going became rough; the path petered out, and I found myself deep in amongst crags. Some anxious scrambling brought me on to the ridge which connects Ben Aden with Sgurr na Ciche, and I was tempted to backtrack and bag that top as well, but, this being the last day out, I was tied to time, and was anxious to get Sgurr na Ciche below my boots before the day grew much older.

I was now on top of Meall a Choire Dhuibh, and the northeast ridge of Ciche rose fiercely ahead, the summit capped in cloud. Thankfully, the ridge was not difficult, and as I approached the cloud level, I found a broken stone wall and the vestiges of a track winding up the steep rocky final section. It was an unexpectedly easy ascent, and I felt convinced that Sgurr na Ciche must be keeping her real reputation as a rugged difficult hill for the descent. I sat by the trig point hoping for the cloud to clear, but soon felt cold in the damp clingy mist. The problem was now to reach the col between Ciche and her neighbour, Garbh Chioch Mhor, for the eastern and southeastern slopes of this summit are notoriously steep. My first attempt brought me to the edge of some very precipitous crags, so back I went to the summit for another try. This time I went more to the left. Success. With a little struggle, I succeeded in making a rather laborious and undignified scramble over the rocks, and managed to reach the col in one piece. Continuing in a south-west direction, I began to climb again, past a small lochan, and on to the summit ridge of Garbh Chioch Mhor. A great rocky corrie opened up on my left, and to the right, steep grassy slopes led down to the Mam na Cloich Airde track. Sadly, time was beginning to get the edge on me, so I didn't carry on eastwards to Sgurr nan Coireachan, another Munro, but simply dropped slowly and carefully down the long slopes to the track, and the 4-mile walk back down to Glendessary and my awaiting car.

Knoydart had been stupendous. Seton Gordon had exaggerated (perhaps he caught it on a bad day) and Bill Murray had been dead right. I had enjoyed four memorable days of gloriously slow and sometimes strenuous effort, but my Knoydart trip had been almost incomparable. The gauntlet of

Knoydart had been taken up and met, and it had been more than hospitable to me. The spell had been cast, and that lonely peninsula of Knoydart, lying so precariously between heaven and hell, will forever be one of my favourites.

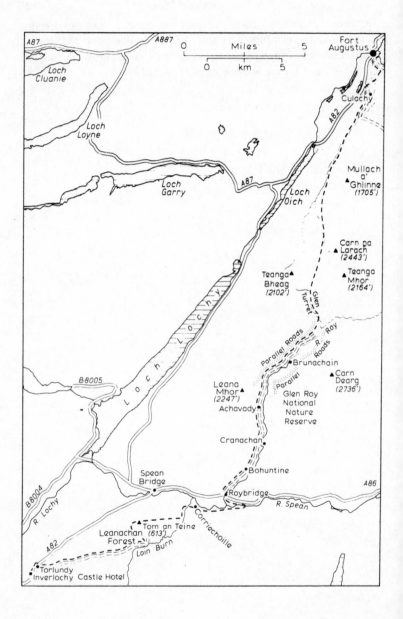

ROUTE 6: IN THE FOOTSTEPS OF MONTROSE

About 38 miles. A two-camp historical walk following the steps of the Royalist army led by the Marquis of Montrose in the winter march preceding the Battle of Inverlochy in 1645.

Maps required: O.S. 1:50,000 Second Series. Sheets 34, 41.

From Fort Augustus walk S.E. across bridge over the R. Tarff to minor road which runs S.W. to Ardachy Lodge, $\frac{3}{4}$ mile. Cross the bridge and take the estate road which runs eventually to Culachy House. Bear left at each path junction and follow path which runs above the Culachy Falls in a S.W. direction. Continue through the glen south-westwards, below the ridge of Druim Laragon and down into Glen Buck. Keep high above the ravine which contains the Calder Burn and continue on path S., until it begins to swing S.W. Leave the path then, and ford the Allt a Ghlinne, before dropping downhill to Glenbuck House. Camp in woods above house or in vicinity. Ask permission at Culachy. Follow long slopes S. between Beinn Bhan and Carn na Larach over the Teanga plateau, and then down slope in a southerly direction into Glen Turret. Follow path into Glen Roy, and follow road which runs in a S.W. direction for 9 miles to Roybridge. Camp at campsite in Roybridge, or wild with permission. Cross R. Spean by footbridge 1 mile E. of village, and follow track westwards for 2 miles to Corriechoille. Take minor road to Killiechonate and follow forest road beside the Cour burn in a southerly direction for 1 mile. Turn due W. through trees and take forest track for 2 miles before turning S.E. to Leanachan, $\frac{3}{4}$ mile. From Leanachan take forest road due W. for $2\frac{1}{4}$ miles to cement works at Creag Aoil, then public road for 2 miles to Torlundy. Cross bridge to A82(t), and follow main road S.W. for 1 mile to Inverlochy.

The Scots novelist John Buchan once related a conversation he had with a famous French general. Discussing the great soldiers that Britain had produced over the years, the Frenchman told him how remarkable it was to him that each part of the British Isles had produced one of four outstanding generals. For England he gave Marlborough, for Ireland, the great Wellington, and for Wales, perhaps surprisingly to some, Oliver Cromwell, who was of course on his father's side a Williams, and of Welsh extraction. With mounting curiosity, Buchan asked about Scotland. The Frenchman looked surprised. "Scotland?" he said, "Can there be any doubt? Have you not the great Montrose?"

James Graham, fifth Earl of Montrose, known in Highland Scotland in the seventeenth century as An Greumach Mor (the Big Graham), was perhaps the greatest military figure thrown up by the Civil War, surpassing even the great Cromwell himself as a general of military genius. It was as a master of mobile guerrilla warfare that Montrose succeeded, leading troops of mainly Highland clansmen and Irish gallowglasses under the captaincy of Colkitto, Alastair Macdonald of Colonsay, over vast tracts of roadless mountain terrain to surprise his enemies. Many of his finest victories were more of an endurance test for his force than proof of their fighting skills, and the combination of his great leadership and the hardy toughness of his men, proved highly successful time after time.

I arrived by bus from Fort William in Kilchumin, nowadays known as Fort Augustus, on a wet dreich afternoon in early February. I had long been fascinated by the events leading up to the Battle of Inverlochy in 1645, which was, arguably, Montrose's greatest victory. Not only did he defeat a considerably larger force than his own, but he had force-marched a battle-tired army almost 40 miles over stormy winter hills to outflank and defeat his great enemy, Macaillein Mor, Archibald Campbell, the Duke of Argyll.

It was my intention to backpack over the exact route that

Montrose had taken, at the same time of year, from Fort Augustus to Fort William, and perhaps experience at first hand something of the hardships and difficulties this great force had to endure. It would also, I hoped, tell me something of this great commander, and the troops he inspired, traditional fighting men, who, in the years to come, were to form the great Highland regiments who fought with distinction and courage in the world's great battles.

Complete with modern tent, sleeping-bag, waterproofs, ice axe and lightweight petrol stove, I was most definitely at a greater advantage than Montrose and his men, and, in the event, I was luckier than them in experiencing fairly benign weather. But the Highland troops of mainly Clans Donald, Stewart and Cameron had a far greater incentive to reach Inverlochy than I did. Theirs was a gut reaction of hatred; they were approaching their ancient enemy the Campbells, and this fact alone, more than any political motive, drove them on through the sleet and the snow and the driving winds, with only an irregular provision of oatmeal and water to sustain them.

James Graham, ironically, was amongst the first earls of Scotland to sign the National Covenant, and even led the Covenant Forces in the hope of preventing Charles I from pushing the Divine Right of Kings too far. However, when he had cause to believe that the Covenanters' support of the English Parliament against the King was being pushed to the point of rebellion, he defected from the ranks of the Covenanters, and after a time, became Charles's most loyal subject in Scotland, and his lieutenant.

The Marquis of Montrose arrived in Kilchumin at the foot of Loch Ness on the evening of 30th January 1645, after having spent the latter months of 1644 plundering the lands of the overlord of the Covenant Estates, the Duke of Argyll. His army had sacked Inveraray and the rich lands of Argyllshire, as Macaillean Mor had made good his escape seaward, in a fishing boat. While the Highlanders enjoyed what to them was a land of milk and honey, word went out to Edinburgh, and forces were sent northwards to try and seal off any route which Montrose might make in that direction.

Montrose knew that the Earl of Seaforth had arrived in Inverness to do battle with him, and was preparing his army for the tussle when he received graver tidings. Ian Lom Macdonald, the Bard of Keppoch (later to become Poet Laureate under Charles II, the first and last poet writing in the Gaelic to be so honoured), arrived in great haste to warn Montrose that Argyll has resurrected his army, and, under the military leadership of Sir Duncan Campbell of Auchinbreck, the best soldier that Clan Campbell could boast, had mustered at Inverlochy (just north of where Fort William stands today) behind the Royalist army. Ian Lom greatly feared that Montrose would be attacked from both north-east and south-west. Montrose knew that Seaforth boasted some 5000 men, mostly peasants, drovers and old soldiers from the garrison at Inverness. Campbell, on the other hand, according to Ian Lom Macdonald, had an army of 3000 soldiers, all experienced and highly skilled under the leadership of that fine and famous warrior Auchinbreck. The Graham knew that the fighting spirit of the Clan Diarmid, as the Campbells were known, was equal to any, and that they were motivated by a lust for revenge for the burning of their Inveraray homes. The Royalist Army of 1500 was caught between two vastly superior forces.

It was now that Montrose showed his skill and bravery as a general. Electing to meet the greater peril first, he called his lieutenants to him. Ian Lom Macdonald would act as guide, to conduct the army over a tract of land the like of which no other army would have dared to march, over the wind-scoured and snow-covered hills between the Great Glen and Glen Spean, to attempt to outflank Argyll and take the Covenant army by total surprise. To do this effectively, it was necessary for the Royalist force to stay high in the hills as much as possible, at all times attempting to keep out of sight and earshot of any Campbell scouting patrols.

Early in the morning of 31st January 1645, the march began, an outflanking movement which was to become one of the greatest exploits in British military history. The old Bard of Keppoch led the plaid-wrapped men out of Kilchumin into the valley of the Tarff, where three of the force were almost immediately drowned attempting to ford the raging and swollen river, an inauspicious start to the manoeuvre.

I left Fort Augustus later in the day, well after noon, after waiting for the village shop to open after lunch so that I could buy some matches, which I had stupidly forgotten. I took the main road south-eastwards, to where a minor road runs to Ardachy Lodge, and, to my relief, a bridge over the River Tarff, near the spot where Montrose lost the first of his men. The river was well and truly swollen today as well, after a mild spell which had all but stripped the higher hills of snow. It would have been a hazardous business to try and ford it, and my inclination to follow the footsteps of Montrose as precisely as possible vanished as fast as the current. I was quite happy to cross the river by the bridge.

Leaving the road a few hundred yards beyond, a track runs through the oak woods towards Culachy House, but by bearing right at each path junction, the house can be avoided. The right path climbs up to higher ground near to where the Culachy River crashes down its steep hanging valley into the waters of the Tarff. The track is a good one, originally constructed by General Wade, but, unfortunately, it didn't last long enough. Beyond a small cottonweed-fringed lochan, it hairpinned eastwards, to run eventually through to the wilds of Badenoch by way of the Corrieyairack Pass to Laggan. There is a little uncertainty among the various authorities as to where Montrose went from here; some have said that he followed the route of the Corrieyairack over the maze of snow-covered hills to the head of the pass at 2500 feet, to the source of the River Spey, and then by way of a pass between the Spey and the

River Roy, descending thus to Glen Spean and the northern foothills of the massive Grey Corries and Ben Nevis mountain ranges to Inverlochy. Both Buchan, and Nigel Tranter who wrote the historical novels *The Young Montrose* and *Montrose, The Captain General*, believe that the route taken was by way of the Tarff, crossing below Culachy, and then parallel to the present A82 and so to Glen Buck and Glen Turret before turning south-west into Glen Roy and then Glen Spean. This route, in fact, is the one documented in the ancient Clanranald Manuscript, and so, the one which I was inclined to follow. The Corrieyairack route would have taken Montrose too far east over unnecessary high ground. It was his intention merely to avoid detection, and this he could have done adequately by crossing the high ground to Glen Buck, taking care to bypass the village of Aberchalder, where Campbell scouts were already searching.

Beyond the Corrieyairack track, a little glen leads through to Glen Buck. The Royalist Army kept to the high ground of Meall a'Cholumain and Druim Laragon before dropping steeply into Glen Buck, but I kept to the glen floor where, although very boggy in places, it was relatively sheltered from the wind-driven rain and sleet which even down here was stinging my cheeks. Working my way through dripping wet forestry plantations, I reached the watershed of the glen, and followed a meandering stream over a bulldozed track which ran, I thought, too high along the eastern slopes of Glen Buck, and down a deep narrow valley into the heavily wooded ravine of Glen Buck. I hadn't realized from the map just how precipitous these slopes were. I had hoped to ford the Calder Burn which flows through Glen Buck, to reach a bulldozed track on the western bank of the burn, but this was now out of the question. The burn, when I could glimpse it through the trees in the ravine, was more of a raging torrent, roaring brown with peat stain, so I climbed back up the slopes again, slipping and sliding on some old snow patches, back onto the bulldozed track which I had earlier spurned.

The sleet had now stopped, which was a blessing, and the cold breeze had begun tearing large rents in the overcast sky. The track was a good one, and now that I was settling into my stride, I began to enjoy the views down the glen towards the high ground which separates Glen Buck from Glen Turret. Six or seven miles had passed since leaving Fort Augustus, and it wouldn't be long until it was dark. My plan was to camp somewhere at the head of Glen Buck, preferably sheltered by the trees, but it was already becoming dark, the time just after 4 p.m. The bulldozed track had petered out into a mere path, boggy and full of puddles, and in places indistinct, and as it began to swerve south-eastwards into the valley of the Allt a Ghlinne, I wasn't at all sorry to leave it and drop down into the glen floor beside the infant Calder Burn. I forded the Allt a Ghlinne comfortably, wading through the shin-deep waters hoping that my gaiters would repel most of it, which they did, and a short walk took me to the old house at Glenbuck. It was getting pretty dark now, and I was groping my way around in the light of a head-torch trying to find a decent sheltered spot to pitch the tent. Much of the ground was saturated, and one or two flat spots which I thought would be ideal, turned out to be virtually quagmires, but I groped my way onwards, wandering uphill, the narrow beam of my head-torch throwing a bright circle through the dark. I could hear, rather than feel, the wind shrieking through the trees above me, and one or two stars twinkled out of the inky black sky. I began to enjoy this dark journey, and felt almost disappointed when I stumbled across a ledge of level, dry grass, not too far from the stream, and sheltered by an indentation in the line of pine trees.

The rain started as I awkwardly put the tent up in the dark, so it was good eventually to crawl into my sleeping-bag and light a candle. With the light flickering and throwing long shadows on the walls of the tent, I cooked a meal, and read the evening away, enjoying Nigel Tranter's account of Montrose's walk in *The Young Montrose*. Up here, on the actual route over which Montrose led his Highland army, I felt almost a part of the story, rather than a fascinated outsider.

Daylight had found the Royalist Army in Glen Buck, a long hard day in front of them before they were to get any rest. John Buchan, in his biography of Montrose, claims that the weather on the high hills had been deathly cold, and the march had been through a "Hyperborean hell". The upper glens were choked with drifting snow, and the rocks glazed with ice, impassable save to Highland brogues.

The climb out of Glen Buck involved a long steady plod over wet ground, a stoical effort by the bare-legged short-kilted clansmen, but easy enough for me wrapped up in modern waterproofs. I had slept late after a cold night, and in the grey dawn of a damp winter morning it took the stimulant of a good breakfast and several brews before I was prepared to exchange the snugness of my sleeping-bag for whatever the day was prepared to throw at me.

To the south, long slopes led up to a murky-looking bealach between Beinn Bhan and Carn na Larach; low clouds hung dreichly and wet slobbery snow made the going slow and difficult. Without the benefit of a Keppoch guide I had to resort to map and compass, following a red needle for some two miles through a world of cheerless grey. Ian Lom Macdonald found his way across this high tableland purely by instinct; according to accounts of the time blizzards raged, the going was painfully slow, and wind-driven sleet and snow made visibility almost nil. Montrose, happy enough in the fact that there could be no Campbell patrols in these inhospitable wastes, hurried his men along, the Royal Standard wrapped around his shoulders, chiding the slower men with his own show of courage and endurance. Remember too that James Graham was well bred and used to a life of relative ease and comfort, unlike his forces of wild Highlanders and Irish gallowglasses who were used to the outdoor life, men of inbred stamina. His own performance was therefore all the more astonishing, his will to succeed on behalf of a weak king only matched by the centuries-old hatred the Macdonalds, Camerons and Stewarts had for Clan Diarmid, the strongest and most powerful family in Scotland.

At last the peat hag-ridden and slush-covered plateau gave way to downward slopes, at first gradual and then more steep as I entered the little valley of Glen Turret, an offshoot of the winding Glen Roy. Descending below the cloud level I saw a narrow valley with a flat bottom, and across the glen the strange lines of the Parallel Roads. These extraordinary terraces contour both sides of Glen Roy, and are thought to be the successive beach levels of some ancient loch which filled Glen Roy towards the close of the Ice Age. Three very distinct terraces run along each side of the glen, the ones on the east side of the glen being more pronounced. The grass and bracken of the "roads" stand out clearly against the heather-covered hillside.

The Royalist Army followed one of the Parallel Roads. Although covered in deep snow it made at least a flat surface to walk on, so the men didn't have to slip and slide on the snowy hillside. Anxious to follow in their steps, I crossed the tumultuous River Turret at Turret Bridge, built by General Wade, soaked to the thighs after wading through wet slush-covered heather. I was later ironically amused to discover that Glen Turret is taken from the Gleann Turraid, meaning "dry glen". Crossing the hillside above Brae Roy Lodge, an old shooting lodge, I reached the first of the "roads" only to find it vanished after a few yards; indeed it was hard at times to distinguish between it and the multitude of sheep tracks which thread the hillside hereabouts. After some abortive attempts at keeping in a straight line, I abandoned the romantic notion of following the Ice Age beach line and took a practical course on to the road which coils its way up the glen from Roybridge. This is a narrow single-track tarmac road, originally built as a bridle path by General Wade and his soldier navvies in the first half of the eighteenth century, although it was almost certain that some sort of track existed before then. Glen Roy was well populated then, and the inhabitants were none too pleased at their glen being made more accessible to English troops! Lower down the glen the road runs high above the tree-lined riverbank, probably an attempt by Wade to avoid the problem of being ambushed by local objectors. Conservationists in those far-off days made their feelings quite obvious.

In high summer this is a busy little road with visitors driving up the glen to view the Parallel Roads in the Glen Roy National Nature Reserve. At this time of the year though, I virtually had it to myself. With the sheep for company I wandered down the empty glen, enjoying the views over to the three great corries which form the far hillside, Coire na Reinich, Coire Bhrunachan (Coire Dubh on the O.S. 1:50,000 map) and Coire Chouplaig, an excellent example of the archetypal hanging valley. In the days when people ground their own oatmeal, Coire Bhrunachan was known for its supply of quern-stones, a softish stone with hard protruding garnets which ground the oats into fine oatmeal.

I stopped briefly at an old derelict house marked on the map as Achavady. It was here that an old resident of Glen Roy, Iain Odhar, reputedly shot the last wolf in the area, giving the flats around the house their name of Achadh a'Mhadaidh, the Field of the Fox, or Wolf. Montrose stopped here too, for three or four hours, to give his exhausted and frozen men a brief respite in their continuous struggle against the elements. Several young deer were shot, and the blood lapped and raw meat eaten by the starving clansmen, wrapped in soaking wet plaids, forbidden by the commander to light even a small warming fire. Ian Lom begged Montrose to push on to his croftship of Keppoch, a mere five or six miles down the glen by Roybridge, where his chief, MacDonald of Keppoch, himself a veteran of the Royalist Army, would make Montrose more than welcome with shelter and provisions. But the Graham refused. Not wishing to insult the sacred offer of hospitality, he carefully explained that his force must, at all costs, avoid all forms of township or croft for fear of treason; it would take only one traitor, one misinformed zealot, to carry word to Argyll at Inverlochy, and the all-important element of surprise would be lost. At the risk of possibly offending Keppoch, the force left Glen Roy high on the slopes of Maol Ruadh, and crossed the raging River Spean at Corriechoille, almost 2 miles west of Roybridge.

I had no need to avoid civilization, on the contrary I needed it. Somehow I had lost the box of matches I had bought in Fort Augustus. So, rather than avoid Roybridge, I made directly down to it on the road, almost having to run the last 2 or 3 miles down the road to catch the shop before it closed.

I camped beyond the railway station, down near the River Spean. It was a cold night with a tingling frost in the air, and it looked very much as though the mild spell was over. The sky was clear, and the moon was pale and encircled by a vivid halo. Montrose had forded the stream at Corriechoille, downriver from here, but unfortunately, there wasn't a bridge there now. With the temperature now plummeting fast towards zero, I had no intention of wading the river come morning. The O.S. map, though, showed that there was a bridge some three-quarters of a mile east of where I was camped. Before I turned in, I investigated, a delightful mid-evening amble on a splendid starlit night. Sure enough, the bridge was still there, and would take me across to the Corriechoille side of the river in the morning.

And so it did. A clear frosty night developed into a fine crystal-sharp morning, the type of winter morning which stings the nostrils with the cold and nips and hurries you through the morning chores to get you on your way. Strangely enough, Montrose had a good day before he attacked the Campbells at Inverlochy, although he had marched through the night before camping at Torlundy, just out of sight of the Campbell camp.

I bustled off over my bridge, and then westwards along a footpath beside the river, past a farmhouse at Insh, and on to the bridge over the Cour Burn at Corriechoille itself. Across the burn, a field separated me from the footpath I wanted. This runs from the farmhouse at Killiechonate, up the left bank of the Cour Burn, and into the great Leanachan Forest.

Some authorities, including Keltie in *History of the Scottish Highlands*, make reference to Montrose taking his army over the Lairig Leacach to the head of Glen Nevis, south of the great long ridge of the Grey Corries, the Aonachs and Ben Nevis itself. Neil Munro, in his novel *John Splendid*, also believes this was the route taken by the Royalist Army. It seems unlikely though; in the first place, for men in this weary, well-nigh exhausted state, such a detour could have taken longer than a day; secondly, Montrose had expert guides in the Camerons and Macdonalds who knew this area flanking Ben Nevis like the back of their hands. Dr Cameron Millar's paper "Montrose in Lochaber" takes the view that it was along the northern flanks of the Grey Corries that Montrose marched, through the great forests of Leanachan. This was also John Buchan's view in his biography of Montrose. It suited me well enough too.

Modern forestry tracks took me to Leanachan itself, where another track ran due west alongside the Allt an Loin. It was in this vicinity that Montrose's advance party almost ran into trouble; a foraging party of Campbells had camped for the night under the trees, the glow from their camp fires giving away their presence. The poor fellows had an inglorious end, cut down by the Royalist advance party as they rose from their plaids. It was death for all of them, Patrick Graham of Inchbrakie, known as Black Pate, insisting that none should escape to raise the alarm. It was but a minor skirmish, but it had a heartening effect on the vanguard of the host. First blood of the contest fell to the Royalists.

My forest track ran in a straight line to the River Lundy and Torlundy, the last 2 miles from Creag Aoil, and the cement factory, on tarmac roads. All along the track occasional views could be glimpsed through the thick forest to the high tops and corries of the Aonachs and Ben Nevis, its north-east-facing cliffs plastered in snow. Along the road I went, enjoying this forest walk with the tantalizing brief glimpses of the high tops, past some forestry houses, over a hump-backed bridge, and I was at Torlundy. The view from here is blocked by plantations, but in 1645, the Great Glen would be seen stretching away in the distance, north-east of the great sea loch of Linnhe, while 2 miles to the south-west of Torlundy, by the banks of the River Lochy at the edge of the vast flats of Corpach Moss, lay the gaunt towers of Inverlochy Castle. An Inverlochy Castle is marked on the O.S. 1:50,000 map, but this is a newer building, a Victorian mansion, nowadays a hotel, which adopted the name of Inverlochy Castle from the old ruins which lie south west of it.

The Royalist Army arrived here in late afternoon; fatigued, sodden through and starving, after accomplishing the almost impossible. It was a feat worthy of the ancient Fingalian legends, a Homeric deed unrivalled in British military history. In forty hours, this army of 1500 men had struggled almost the same number of miles, in atrocious conditions, an outflanking manoeuvre to surprise their great enemy. Black Pate's advance party crept through the trees to spy the scene. Across the great flood plain, the semi-ruinous fort of Inverlochy rose from its grassy mound among the reeds, and all around, the pavilions and camp fires of the Campbell host. The desperate journey had not been in vain, the Campbells were still there, unsuspecting.

After another long night shivering in the open, Montrose placed his army in a long line southwards over the lower slopes of Meall an t-Suidhe, the western outlier of Ben Nevis. In a thin cold drizzle, as the Campbells were lighting their morning fires, the surrounding mountains echoed to the fierce notes of bugles and the mighty yells and screams of the Celtic host. To the accompaniment of the Cameron pibroch "Sons of Dogs, Come and I will Give You Flesh", the Royalists attacked and the great force of the Campbells was routed; the Duke of Argyll himself once again escaping seaward in his galley. Half the Covenanting army was killed, to only four of the Royalists. The great clan power of the Campbells was destroyed at a stroke. After Inverlochy they never recovered as a true fighting force and, at last, the heather of the Macdonald badge overcame the bog myrtle of the Campbells.

Montrose, though, paid dearly for his victory. The long arduous march had taken its toll on his son, who died some months later from pneumonia and exhaustion. In two years, Montrose won six brilliant victories against the Covenanters, and the country lay as his for the taking on behalf of Charles I. But, just as it was the Highlanders who had won the country for him, so it was they who finally let him down. Long-neglected crofts and farms had the clansmen drifting home to attend to their families and crofts. With the Campbells defeated, the motivation to march and fight on was largely gone, and domestic matters became more important than any political cause. In September, Montrose's badly reduced army was slaughtered at Philiphaugh near Selkirk, and five years later, after another attempt to win Scotland for the Crown, James Graham was betrayed by MacLeod of Assynt in Sutherland, taken to Edinburgh and hanged, while his old enemy, Archibald Campbell, looked on from behind a curtain.

I wandered down the road to take a look at the ruins of the once proud castle. Now, neighboured by the British Rail Goods Yard, much of its pride has gone, and its remains are cared for by the Department of the Environment. The route of the great march is still there to be enjoyed though, as are the words of the Bard of Keppoch, Montrose's guide through those terrible hours in the snows and the driving wind:

'twas I that led the highland host,
through wild Lochaber's snows,
What time the plaided clans came down,
To battle with Montrose,
I've told you how the Southrons fell,
Beneath the broad claymore,
And how we smote the Campbell clan,
By Inverlochy's shore.

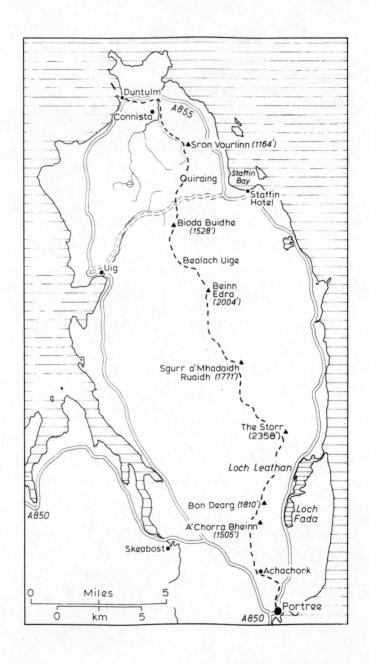

On the Trotternish Ridge in Skye

The Storr Rock on the Trotternish peninsula

Blair Castle: the beginning of Comyn's Road

On Comyn's Road, leaving the Whim Plantation

Gaick Lodge

Ruthven Barracks: the culmination point of Comyn's Road

An Teallach from the Destitution Road

Lord Berkeley's Seat appears through the gloom

On the ridge of Beinn Tarsuinn

Beinn a'Chlaidheimh, Sgurr Ban and Mullach Coire Mhic Fhearchair
from Beinn Tarsuinn

Looking west over the Great Wilderness from A'Mhaighdean

Winter walker

ROUTE 7: TROTTERNISH IN SKYE

About 30 miles. An easy one-camp high-level walk over the backbone of the Trotternish Peninsula in northern Skye, from Duntulm in the north to Portree in the south.

Map required: O.S. 1:50,000 Second Series. Sheet 23.

From Duntulm, take A855 road E. for $1\frac{3}{4}$ miles, then follow farm road S. for $\frac{3}{4}$ mile to Connista. Leave the road and follow Kilmaluag river for about 500 yards, then Lon Horro burn S.E. for 1 mile into Coire Mhic Eachainn. Ascend western slopes of Sron Vourlinn to summit. Follow ridge S. for $\frac{1}{4}$ mile, the S.W. for 200 yards, before dropping down steep grassy rakes to E. to arrive in trench which runs N./S. to the E. of the cliff face. Follow this trench S. for $\frac{3}{4}$ mile, before ascending into Quiraing by obvious gaps in the cliff face. Descend from Quiraing to good path which runs S.W. past the Prison to the minor Staffing-Uig road, 1 mile. Climb slopes to S. of road to Bioda Buidhe, and follow ridge S.W., for $\frac{1}{2}$ mile, then S. curving S.E. to Druim na Coille, $1\frac{1}{4}$ miles, then over Bealach Uige and up slopes of Beinn Edra. Descend slopes of Edra to S., climb top marked on map as 528 metre spot height, and drop down below Bealach Amadal for camp. Ascend Groba nan Each, and follow obvious ridge S.E., then E.S.E. to Sgurr a Mhadaidh Ruaidh. Return to main ridge and walk due S. over minor tops to Hartaval, before turning S.E. to climb steep slopes of the Storr. From cairn, follow S.S.W. direct to Bealach Beag, then S.S.W. to Bealach Mor, where a good sheep track runs from below the E. facing cliffs, due S., bypassing the intervening cliff face of Ben Dearg. Follow this path S. past Beinn Mheadhonach, and A Chorra-bheinn. Take bearing due S. over moorland to Achachork, where a minor road runs S.E. to A855, the S. by road to Portree.

It was on a June day of blustery winds and rain storms that Harry MacShane and I turned our backs on the advancing veils of grey showers which were sweeping across the Minch from the purple hills of Harris, to walk south over the spine of the Trotternish peninsula in northern Skye. This walk, from the old castle of Duntulm to Portree, the capital of the Isle of Skye, is in my opinion without equal in the whole of Scotland. A glance at the Ordnance Survey map of northern Skye will show you the great feature of Trotternish; a long winding escarpment of basalt cliffs running in a southerly direction from the steep peaks of Sgurr Mhor and Sron Vourlinn near Duntulm, to the bare moorland above Portree.

The sheer east-facing cliffs of this great ridge are sills, or sheets of lava, immensely thick, intruded between the upper and lower layers of the basalt plateaux, after they were laid down. The upper basalt sheets have been cut back to the ridge, and have left the long intrusive sills in a long line from Portree, up the length of the peninsula, and out to sea as far north as the Shiant Isles. While the east-facing cliffs are sheer, the western slopes of the ridge are in complete contrast. Long gentle grassy slopes run all the way to the rim of the cliffs, the turf shorn short and smooth by the continual grazing of sheep and rabbits, and by the constant caress, and occasional battering, of the westerly breezes. The summits of the ridge are not high, reaching 2358 feet above sea level at the trig point on the Storr, but on a clear day these lowly hills offer superb panoramas from as far west as St Kilda, beyond the Outer Hebrides, over the jagged outline of Skye's chief attraction, the Cuillin, to the great mountain masses of Torridon, Gareloch and Applecross on the mainland.

These hills perhaps lack the excitement of a Mamore ridge, and by no stretch of the imagination can you experience here the lonely desolation of Knoydart or Fisherfield, but the easy undulating walking, in continual view of the sea all around you, has a charm of its own. The salt air is vibrant and heady, the short turf makes the physical effort of walking a joy, and the tiny dots of whitewashed cottages and the tracings of green fields on the moors below add a strong sense of human interest to the beauty of nature. In springtime and early summer a profusion of wild flowers decorates the predominant greenery, with the very rare *Koenigia islandica* (Icelandic purslane) growing on some of the slopes, and one is in the constant company of birds: wheatears, dippers, snipe, pipits, plovers, and of course gulls, lots of them.

But the delights of Trotternish are not purely pastoral and gentle. At the north of the peninsula, opposite Staffin Bay, the wild towers and crazy pinnacles which form the battlements of the Quiraing, a collapsed lava slip, present an eerie prospect, while further south, below the frowning cliffs of the Storr, another slip has culminated in the weird formations of the Old Man of Storr and his neighbours, eroded basaltic columns which throw their great spires skywards in a jumble of ghostly pinnacles.

There can be few places in Scotland as exciting, on a day of crashing surf and billowing strom-cloud, as Duntulm Castle. Clinging to the rocky headland rising sheer from the restless waters of the Minch, the grey ruins show a brave face to the wrath of the north-westerly gales. It is in an exposed position, on the north-western tip of the peninsula, but, as the ancient stronghold of the Macdonalds of the Isles, its exposure was its strength. From here, the kings of the isles could taunt their enemies and, summoning their forces, sally forth on their war galleys to do battle by sea and defend their sovereignty against the rival kings of Scotland.

> Ged tha thu'n diugh 'a d'aibheas fhuar,
> Bha thu uair 'a d'aros righ.
>
> (Though thou art today a ruin cold,
> Thou wert once the dwelling of a king.)

Duntulm was certainly a "ruin cold" today, as the winds scurried off the sea, and discouraged any temptation to linger. In between grey showers, a strong sun burst from the fast-moving clouds, dazzling off the green waters, and intensifying the colours of the pebbly bays and the distant hues of the hills of Harris. We had driven north to Duntulm from Portree, up the west coast of the peninsula of Trotternish via Uig. Harry had left his car in the square in Portree, awaiting our return.

From the ruins of the castle, we followed the scenic road eastwards for some 2 miles, through the scattered croftship of Kilmaluag, to where a minor road turned off due south to a croft marked on the O.S. map as Connista. Low-lying thatched cottages made an attractive foreground to the bare moorland, backed by the looming cliffs of Sgurr Mhor and Sron Vourlinn. The prominent nose of Vourlinn was our first objective, the beginnings of the long series of cliffs which would carry us down to Portree. We hoped to camp high on the ridge somewhere, and carried a two-man tent and enough food for two days. With the prospect of an idyllic campsite, we had stowed away a flask of whisky and a couple of cigars, little titbits of delight which add a touch of luxury to even the finest of campsites.

Sron Vourlinn is known locally as Sron Bhiornal, after a Norse princess who once lived on the island. Before she died, she asked that she might be buried high on the hills so that her tomb might look across the sea towards Norway. There is nothing on the hill to mark her grave, but it is claimed that she was laid to rest on a grassy ledge on the cliff, about seventy feet below the crest of the hill. It was an easy walk across the moor to the great corrie Coire Mhic Eachainn, which separates Vourlinn from Sgurr Mhor. The climb is gradual, with several patches of peat bog to negotiate, but our attention was constantly held by the harsh crying of snipe, protesting at our disturbance, the bustle of dippers on the fast-flowing streams, and the outpourings of joyous song from tiny skylarks. Gradually, the slope became steeper, and we passed from bog-cotton-strewn wetlands to springy cropped turf. In a very short time, we stood at the crumbling edge of the precipice; one moment easy-angled slope, the next moment a void! This is the great feature of these ridges: the dramatic contrast from moorland bare and featureless to these great cliffs, often overhanging and always high, falling sheer to a shallow valley below, sprinkled with glinting lochans and prickled with jagged volcanic upthrusts. Away behind us in the green waters of the Minch, the Island of Trodday lay close to the shore; beyond it the outline of the distant Shiant Isles, and even further away, the sun just catching the sea cliffs of Lewis. The peaks on the Scottish mainland were visible only as a dark mass; cloud and haze made them indiscernible from here, but in front of us, southwards, the progression of the steep noses of the escarpment flowed on like the crests of giant waves, towering to the sky, and fading into the haze beyond the splintered outline of the Storr.

From Vourlinn, we followed the crumbling cliff edge south and then south-west until the slopes began to rise towards the craggy outlines of Fir Bhreugach. By following the cliff's edge uphill, we would eventually reach the summit of Meall na Suiramach, the hill which is usually, erroneously, called the Quiraing. The Quiraing (a fold, or pen) is in fact, the name for the collection of spires, rocks and volcanic debris which has been split away from the rock face, and since we were keen to visit this curious amphitheatre, we agreed that the sensible thing to do was to drop down below the level of the escarpment, and enter the Quiraing from below. A slanting grassy shelf led us down through the cliffs, and we quickly reached the floor of this strange hidden valley which runs the length of the escarpment. Sheltered now from the wind, we wandered through a wood of weird spires and bluffs, the remnants of a volcanic age, the great black cliff to our right sombre and dripping wet with running water. Only in volcanic Iceland have I ever seen formations like those below the Quiraing; contorted, bent and strangely malevolent, like crooked fingers of rock beckoning you towards some other world. The mystic quality of the place is further emphasized by the lavish lushness of the slope; wild flowers grow in abundance, the grass is an intense shade of green, which seems to soften the harshness of the landscape; almost to the effect of surrealism.

We lay behind a crumbling wall and soaked in the atmosphere during a brief lunch. Harry was in high spirits. Only a few years before he had lain at death's door after a severe heart attack cut short his career as a consultant engineer. The stresses and strains of being a director of five separate companies had taken their toll, and doctors told him that he would never lead an active life again, but Harry violently abhorred the thought of spending the rest of his life as a semi-invalid. The hills proved to be the only tonic he required. Turning his back on the business world which was almost his downfall, he became warden of Crianlarich Youth Hostel in Perthshire, and now finds complete fulfilment in a simpler and more physically demanding lifestyle, running hill-walking courses, wandering off on week-long backpacking trips, and every now and then visiting coronary patients in hospital to tell them from first-hand experience that their world is not necessarily at an end. I enjoy walking with Harry, and not only because we share a similar humour and outlook. Every minute in the hills, whether it is raining, snowing or blowing half a gale, is savoured to the full by Harry MacShane. The words, "It's great, man", are never far from his lips, and enthusiasm like that is infectious. He has a fitness worthy of a man half his age, and his one and only regret is that he didn't take up backpacking earlier in his life, but, judging from the number of hours he spends in the hills, he is doing all he can to make up for the loss.

Neither of us had visited the Quiraing before, and although we had seen photographs of the place, we were not prepared at all for what lay in store. The normal route into the Quiraing follows a footpath from the Staffin to Uig road, the only east-west road to cross the escarpment. This was a mile or so south of where we were, and being impatient to get to grips with it, we decided to enter by the back door.

A good sheep track follows the base of the cliff southwards, and this we followed for a short distance until we saw that the sheer cliff had become riven and split by great gullies and enormous rifts. This, we realized, was a way into the recesses of the hidden stronghold. We left our rucksacks by the path, and unencumbered, clambered up the green talus slopes and into the shadows of this bewildering jumble of precipices, pinnacles and hollows. Above us, immense crags, blocks and spires loomed high, scree slopes leading us upwards into a giant amphitheatre. Great slices of rock, fissured, weathered and cracked, stood apart from the main cliff behind, and through these great fissures, we could gaze out to the contrasting pastoral scene below; the tiny crofts shrunken to insignificance, the green fields, rolling and soft, and the swell of the sea breaking its surf on the great curve of Staffin Bay. Another surprise awaited us. In this world of Titan verticalities, of grey and black upthrusts, it seemed almost unreal to come across a high rounded table of lush cropped grass, as flat and smooth as a bowling-green, so surely one would think, the work of some supernatural force. This is the Table, the jewel of the Quiraing. A slanting ledge ran on to the surface of this wide upthrust, and behind it, perhaps in sympathy with the lushness of the unexpected turf, the riven cliff face is a veritable rock garden. Yellow globe-flowers, red and white campions, blue butterwort and sprays of golden roseroot offer a splash of colour to the shining black rock; the Hanging Gardens of Babylon couldn't have been finer. Almost to exaggerate the splendour of the place, a heavy silence hung around us. No winds breathed in here, no rustling of grass, no crashing streams; only the sound of our boots and the exclamations of our delight broke the cathedral hush. This we decided, could well have been the setting for Tolkien's Rivendell, home of Elrond and his elvin folk. What a place to spend a contemplative weekend. Harry wanted to camp there and then, but it wasn't yet three o'clock, there was a lack of water and a long distance still ahead of us forced us on. We promised each other a return in the very near future, with an overnight camp in what must be one of the most spectacular settings in Scotland.

We left the Table, down dark corridors of scree, past the highest of all the pinnacles, the towering spire of the Needle, 120 feet in height, tapering both at the top and bottom. More slopes of black scree slid us down to the track in front of the Prison, the southerly outpost of the Quiraing, a massive assemblage of rock like some vast ancient fortress. No one seems to know how this rock came by its name, but it is said that the ghost of some old cleric used to emerge from the rock from time to time, until eventually he was laid to rest by some good and saintly person.

We quickly followed the path back to where our packs lay, then retraced our steps back past the Prison, and along a beautiful terraced track which ran along the top of the slope, just below the foot of the cliffs. Below us the narrow Staffin to Uig road wound its way up to the escarpment, before a couple of very tight hairpin turns lifted it across to the long smooth slopes running down to Uig Bay. Beyond the road, the escarpment nose undulated southwards, as impressive as ever. On the moorland, some crofters were busy "at the peat", digging and cutting the turf into manageable sizes, the long thin strips of their endeavour like little scars on the surface of the moor. We met several other walkers making for the Quiraing from the car-park on the road below; all of them commenting, with a hint of surprise I suspect, on the quality of the views. On an island where the Cuillin Hills are reckoned to be the finest natural feature, many folk are more than a little surprised that there can be such a contrast in the north of the island, where they can view a scene equally impressive. This track is a remarkably beautiful one, with the wide sweep of the shore providing a parallel to the sweeping fringe of the ridge, rising tier upon tier to a height of over 2000 feet, to where the long rim cuts into the sky. Even on an overcast day like ours, the outlook was one of total grandeur, yet soft; a green softness which reminded me strongly of the west coast of County Clare. All that was needed to set the scene was the tinkle of a harp and the melancholy wail of the Uillean pipes.

We didn't dally by the roadside, where a gaggle of motorists were enjoying the scene from the comfort of picnic chairs, but pushed on up the easy slopes of Bioda Buidhe. Now that we were outwith the protection of the Quiraing rock, the strong north-westerly wind, bred and nurtured far out in the solitudes of the Atlantic, gusted us along mercilessly. Below, in the lee of the cliffs, a profusion of rowan trees grew on ledges on the cliff, remarkable in that trees are extremely conspicuous in Trotternish by their almost complete absence. Apart from this long ridge it is an open landscape, exposed to the vagaries of the Atlantic storms, storms which do all in their power to discourage growth. These lonely rowans are the more attractive for it.

Several old hill passes cross this backbone of land from east to west, passes which were all trodden in days gone by, but today echo only to the shouts and whistles of an occasional shepherd. Even walkers are few and far between, most visitors climbing to the Quiraing from their car, before driving south to do the same on the Old Man of Storr. The Bealach nan Coisichean and the Bealach Uige are two of these old passes. Both are low points on the escarpment, at places where the cliff can be negotiated with little difficulty, and below the Bealach Uige, nestling darkly into the rock, lies Loch Corcasgil. One day, so it is said, a shepherd and his wife were on the hill, passing the time by trundling great boulders over the edge of the cliff into the dark waters below. Suddenly, there was a great turmoil in the middle of the loch, and the poor folk saw a huge black horse emerge from the water, and swim to the shore, neighing angrily. The animal, or *each uisge*, a water horse, looked in fury all around, trying to see who had the audacity to disturb him in his lair. The shepherd and his wife, at once recognizing the fearsome steed as the dreaded *each uisge*, a "beastie" with the power to change at will into human form, crouched behind a rock which they had just been about to roll into the loch. With wet gleaming flanks the water horse stood for a while, then with a grunt, sprang back into the lochan and dived below the black waters. The water horse is a common legend in Skye, and a great number of lonely lochans were said to harbour such a beast, so much so that as recently as 1870, attempts were made in dragging lochs to try and capture one of the supernatural breed. Derek Cooper, in his excellent gazetteer of the Isle of Skye, reminds cynics that perhaps they shouldn't condemn the folk of Skye as being too simple and superstitious because of their belief in the *each uisge*. Even today, thousands of pounds are being spent and all the resources of modern science are being used in trying to discover a "beastie" in Loch Ness!

To the south of the Bealach Uige, a fence runs alongside the rim of the cliffs to the summit of Beinn Edra, the second highest point on the ridge at just over 2000 feet. As we climbed the long slopes, we entered a cap of cloud, which, with the north-westerly wind still blowing, made an unwelcome combination of cold and damp. We didn't linger on the summit, as it was almost six o'clock, and our thoughts turned from water horses to thinking about somewhere to camp. Our original plan of camping high on the ridge was now completely out of the question because of the strong wind which was blowing, so we had to find a way down through the cliffs below the wall of the escarpment. Two more humps on the ridge had to be crossed before the steepness and height of the cliff weakened enough to allow a descent. A grassy rake, steep but climbable, allowed us to slither down to some scree slopes, on which we ran with great bounding leaps, the stones and scree sliding down like a grey avalanche. The corrie floor was sheltered from the worst of the wind, but the ground was wet and boggy. With a little searching, we eventually found a small islet of dry turf where we put the tent up, and cooried down inside. Just as we were brewing our first cup of tea, the mist and cloud fell like a heavy grey curtain, and the view out to sea evaporated into a grey shroud. Ah well; we still had the cigars and whisky! We blethered and brewed into the night, and through the pleasant fug we built up in the tent, we took note that the wind was becoming stronger. Every so often we could hear it sweep over the clifftop behind us, drop into the corrie, and rattle and shake the tent for a few minutes, before it died away with a sigh. Fortified by our drams, we fell asleep easily enough; that deep contented sleep of the happy backpacker. (Or perhaps it should be the deep contented sleep of the inebriated backpacker?)

By morning it was windier and cloudier than ever, and to add a touch of misery to the melancholy scene, it was raining too; that unmistakable limp, drenching smir which has been the Skye visitor's curse for generations. Besides Skye's superb scenery, and the hospitality of its inhabitants, the island is universally notable for two other things: the quality of its rain, and midges. By some merciful act, the two very rarely coincide, so I suppose one must take the attitude of being thankful for small mercies.

We packed up our belongings, hoisted our packs on our backs, and scampered back up onto the ridge again, huddled up in our waterproofs like hedgehogs. As we stuck our noses up over the corrie rim, the wind hit us with the force of a piledriver, and it was a hesitant couple of backpackers who made their way south over the Bealach Chaiplin. It was blowing a gale and we were soaked through in no time, but luckily the wind and rain were blowing from behind. All we had to do was keep well away from the edge of the crumbling cliff for fear of a great gust toppling us over. In the gloomy light, the great voids to our left were even more impressive than they had been the day before; mist swirled in the depths below us, and for all we knew, the voids could well have been bottomless, rather than the thousand or so feet which they actually were.

After half an hour or so, as is usually the case on such days, we began to enjoy ourselves again. The struggle against the elements becomes an acceptance of things as they are, and the unhappy sensations of damp clamminess is forgotten once you are warm and on the move; it is only when you stop moving for any length of time that discomfort lays its miserable hand on your shoulder and hurries you on your way again.

The ridge undulated steadily, and we followed the cliff from a respectable distance, watching it appear from the murk, now rising, and then descending in a series of gentle bumps. We climbed on to the nose of Sgurr a Mhadaidh Ruaidh, the Hill of the Red Fox, a name which sounds more evocative in its Gaelic pronunciation. Try "Sgoor a Vaddie Rooa". This was the scene of an exciting children's book written by Allan Campbell MacLean, a story of skulduggery and adventure which was also successfully televised. A descent of the Bealach Hartaval brought us below the cloud level, and allowed us to catch a glimpse of the Storr rocks across a vast deep-set corrie, before steep slopes had us climbing into the murk again on to the summit of Hartaval itself. Many of the place-named in Skye, indeed in all the Hebrides, are, like Hartaval, of Norse origin, and it is claimed that much Norse blood still flows in the veins of the Sgiannaichs. Indeed, it wasn't until the Battle of Largs in 1263 that Norse occupation of these islands was brought to an end, and until then, the Norsemen were settlers in Skye, with much intermarriage taking place between them and the Celts.

When planning this walk, Harry and I hadn't really expected it to be very strenuous, but with the wind and rain, and the continual up and down, we both felt a bit tired by the time we reached the long steep climb up to the Storr, at 2358 feet the highest point in the traverse. Despite being soaked, we "took" ten minutes and huddled up beside the shelter of some large rocks in the Bealach a'Chuirn, between Hartaval and Storr. We ate a quick lunch of cheese and chocolate, and drank in the long views down to the west, by Loch Snizort and away across Vaternish to the distant outlines of MacLeod's Tables. The wind continued to gust the clouds across the face of the Storr, now and then lifting the curtain up high enough to allow us a brief peep at the summit, and then dropping again just as suddenly.

We struggled up through the yo-yoing clouds, and reached

the trig point on the summit in a brief moment of clarity. Away below, the spires of the pinnacles reached towards us through flitting mists, the Old Man, the largest, unfortunately just out of sight. As time was running against us, we decided against clambering down through steep gullies into Coire Faoin, although it was tempting to visit the Old Man of Storr in his impressive stronghold. Unlike the Quiraing, which had been a new experience for both of us, we had visited the Old Man of Storr before, so on this occasion we were well content to shout our renewed greeting from above, before turning west, and then south, around the corrie rim, to descend the grassy slopes to the Bealach Beag.

Below the cloud again, the remainder of our walk stretched out in front. The contrast between the dark bastions and weird summits of Storr, and the countryside to the south, is as acute as that between Quiraing and the lands of Staffin. The Storr lochs, Leathan and Fada, lay like quicksilver, two lochs well stocked with brown trout. The valley lies far below, green and inviting; at its further end lay Portree and the twinkling waters of the bay. To the east is the sea, breaking on the skerries of northern Raasay, and beyond the dim and shadowy outline of the hills of Gareloch. Rona, with her broken rocks, and Raasay of the purple hills lie between here and the mainland, and now and then, as the watery sun tried to ooze from between the scudding clouds, a stray drift of light would shine on the coast of Applecross and the mountains beyond. A narrow sound squeezes its way below Portree beneath the sharp peak of Ben Tianavaig, and then turns southwards towards Broadford, where it becomes lost under the shadow of Scalpa. In that direction, the Red Hills and the black Cuillin should have caught the eye, but alas, this particular day had them swatched in dark cloud, invisible and remote.

Immediately in front, the ridge wound its way slightly south-westwards, over a series of small bumps, before the way became barred by the steep front of Ben Dearg, whose long ridge runs perpendicular to the main one. By this time Harry and I both felt tired and, in an effort to avoid a confrontation with the vertical crags, we cunningly outwitted the contours by dropping down below the ridge from the Bealach Mor, where a terraced sheep track bypassed Ben Dearg and Beinn Mheadhonach behind it, to pick its way through the drumlins to the moorland above Portree. At first I felt a little guilty about forsaking the final tops of the walk, but any apprehension I felt was soon forgotten in the sheer delight of this track. People generally reckon that sheep are daft creatures, but this was the finest engineered sheep track I have ever seen. Running along below the cliffs it passed its way through a veritable garden of blooming wild flowers: chickweed, wintergreen, alpine lady's mantle, mossy cyphel, least cudweed, wild thyme and pearlwort. Even the long ribbons of red scree which hung on the steep slopes were dotted with campions and starry saxifrage, and through this brilliant finery, our sheep track passed its way. Even as the alpines of the slope turned to the cotton grass on the peaty moorland the track kept us straight, before finally fading away as we began to descend from the slopes of A'Chorra-bheinn. It wasn't long before we could see the houses of Portree, the Port of the King, so named after a Royal visit from James V in 1540; and a short walk on a tarmacked road past some modern bungalows took us on to the A855 Portree to Staffin road, a mile or so from the town.

Sherriff Nicolson, the Skye poet, once said: "To ascend Storr and follow the mountain ridge the whole way till you come to the Quiriang, is no doubt one of the grandest promenades in Skye, commanding wide views in all directions." Sceptics say that he never did follow it himself, but the backpacker who does choose to follow it will be amply rewarded. Harry and I were delighted with our walk, and we did not have the joys of "commanding wide views" for much of the time, but before leaving Portree to collect my car back at Duntulm, we promised ourselves a return visit and what will be a memorable camp in that astonishing labyrinth of towers and hollows which make up the Quiraing, a place which surely must be one of the wonders of Scotland.

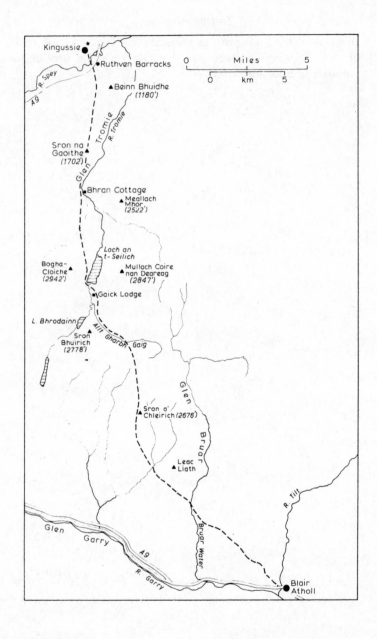

ROUTE 8: COMYN'S ROAD

About 30 miles. A one-camp walk over mixed terrain reaching an altitude of over 2000 feet. Following thirteenth-century road from Blair Atholl to Ruthven near Kingussie.

Maps required: O.S. 1:50,000 Second Series. Sheets 43, 42, 35.

Enter Blair Atholl Estate by main gate 200 yards E. of railway station on A9. Walk N.W. on drive to Blair Castle, then 300 yards N.W. to Old Blair. Follow track by Banvie Burn for 1 mile to edge of Whim Plantation, cross gate, and follow track for 2 miles to Glen Banvie Wood. Leave track on footpath running N.W. for 1 mile to Cuilltemhuc. Strike uphill N.W. for 1 mile to bothy at Clunes and on to track which runs for 1 mile to old shielings at the junction of the Allt a'Chireachain and the All a'Chire Mhoir. Climb N.N.W. on to ridge of Sron a'Chleirich. Climb to summit and follow track N. for 5 miles, over Bac na Creige and down to Allt Gharbh Gaig. Cross footbridge to N. bank and walk N.W. to meet the Gaick track at G.R. 758835, 1½ miles. Camp. Walk N. for ¾ mile to Gaick Lodge, cross river in front of lodge and head N. up pony track on W. side of Loch an t-Seilich climbing steadily to Maol an t-Seilich and down long slopes to Bhran Cottage, 4 miles. Keep to W. bank of R. Tromie and head over Sron na Gaoithe and on to the footpath which runs N., then N.E., before dropping down northwards to Ruthven, 6 miles.

During the past few years, an enormous amount of money has been spent on improving the Perth to Inverness road, the A9, especially the stretch over the Drumochter Pass, thought by many to be dreary, dull and depressing. This part of the road is of great antiquity though, following as it does the route of the Great Highland Road which General Wade built in the eighteenth century, to help quell the rebellious notions of the Highland clans.

Until Wade built his road, the main route through the wild Grampians was by way of a high-level bridleway called the Minigaig, which ran more or less due north from Blair Atholl in Perthshire, to the castle of Ruthven, near the village of Kingussie, in Badenoch. This was the route taken by the cattle drovers and their great herds of hill beasts as they made their yearly journey south to the popular trysts of Crieff and Falkirk. The main highway to the south was over the great wedge of land which lies between the Pass of Drumochter in the west, and the line of Glen Tilt, Glen Geldie and Glen Feshie in the east. Even to this day, the track is complete. Bulldozed for most of its length for estate use, the Minigaig is a recognized right of way, and offers a first-class expedition over a lonely remote area for the walker who seeks solitude and peace.

It was another track, though, even more ancient than the Minigaig, which appealed to my imagination. A sixteenth-century manuscript, MacFarlane's *Geographic Collections*, refers to ''a way from the gate of Blair in Atholl to Ruthven in Badenoch made by David Comyn, for carts to pass with wine and the way is called Rath na Pheny, or way of wagon wheels. It is laid with calsay in sundries parts''.

Tradition claims that a Comyn and his wife were passing through Atholl during the latter half of the thirteenth century, and on their arrival at Kilmaveonaig, on the banks of the River Tilt, went to the inn for refreshments. They were so taken by the quality of the ale, that they asked the landlord where the ingredients came from. The malt, the landlord said, came from Perth, and the water, which gave the ale its special flavour, came from the stream which runs through the village. Comyn decided there and then that he would transport the ale to his castle at Ruthven, and immediately had a road surveyed and built over the pathless tract of wilderness between the two places.

Whether the story that the impulsiveness of Comyn's desire

for Atholl ale led directly to the building of the road which bears his name is historically accurate or not, we do not know. What we do know for certain, is that a highway, known as Rathad nan Cuimeinach, or Road of the Comyns, most certainly existed between Ruthven and Blair Atholl. As sixteenth- and seventeenth-century maps show only the route of the Minigaig, we can assume that Comyn's Road had fallen into disuse by that time, probably because the newer Minigaig route was a few miles shorter.

The advantage of both these routes over the modern road through Drumochter is one of distance; they are both far shorter. From Blair Atholl to Kingussie via Drumochter is 42 miles; Comyn's Road is 30 miles and the Minigaig about 27 miles. Admittedly the older routes would be impassable in winter, as they both climb to an appreciable height above sea level, but this would have been of little consequence in the early days as there was a minimum of travel during these months anyway.

The feasibility of Comyn's Road as a backpacking route implanted itself in my imagination as I traced the old route on the map. The Forests of Atholl and Gaick are vast wild areas, the rounded hills reaching undulating plateaux of over 2000 feet; the streams meander down peaty slopes and corries to lonely glens, and the occasional wild spectacular fissure slashes the bare hillside, to make slopes of broken rock, craggy and rough, laced with roaring waterfalls. There is also a wealth of legends among these hills, where today, the bleat of a lamb or the plaintive call of a whaup echo through the emptied glens which once were alive with the sounds of cattle lowing, the laughing of children, and the singing of the women during the long evenings of the summer shieling.

Blair Atholl and Kingussie, which is only a couple of miles from Ruthven, are both on the main railway line from London to Inverness, an ideal situation which allows the backpacker to travel north to Blair, and then catch the southbound train again from Kingussie at the end of the walk. Living in Aviemore, I

simply left my car in the car-park at Kingussie station, caught
the train to Blair Atholl, and walked back to my car through
Comyn's Road. It is only a 40-minute journey from Kingussie to
Blair Atholl, over the summit of Drumochter Pass, with 3000-
foot-high hills forming the jaws of the pass. I arrived in Blair
Atholl at 10 a.m., on a chilly, cloudy June morning. The old grey
buildings are full of character, although the busy A9 which runs
through the village detracts from any temptation to linger; but
it is the castle, sitting smugly behind the larches and broad
acres of policies between it and the buzzing of the traffic, which
is the real attraction.

Jacket on, rucksack tightened up, I marched up the long
straight drive through the castle grounds, past the caravan site.
Like so many of Britain's stately homes, Blair Castle and its
grounds have been titivated up almost like a park, with ponies,
gardens, nature trails and car parks. It has been tastefully done,
and large display maps are provided to guide you around. The
castle itself has had a chequered history. The oldest part of the
building, Cumming's Tower, was built in 1269 by John Comyn
of Badenoch, and various alterations and additions have been
made since. Edward III visited it in 1336, Mary Queen of Scots
in 1564 and the Marquis of Montrose garrisoned his army in it
in 1644. A less sociable call was made by Oliver Cromwell in
1652, and Claverhouse stayed there before the Battle of
Killiecrankie in 1689. The present resident, the Duke of Atholl,
has the expensive honour of being the only British subject
permitted to retain a private army, the Atholl Highlanders.

Comyn's Road originally began from Kilmaveonaig, where
Comyn reputedly tasted his beer, on the east bank of the River
Tilt. The actual route for the first couple of miles is largely
circumstantial, as forestry, cultivation, and a multitude of tracks
and paths have successfully obscured the original road, but, if
Comyn had indeed built the road to link his castles of Blair and
Ruthven, what better place to start than from the front door of
Blair Castle? I felt slightly conspicuous with shorts, boots and
rucksack, as I mingled with a camera-clutching coach party,

and as it became evident that I was likely to be swept through the front portals of the castle by an exuberant German courier along with the rest of his flock, I thought it was about time that I began my walk.

Leaving the castle steps, I made my way past Diana's Grove, a dark wood which surrounds a statue of the Greek goddess, to Old Blair, where a track strikes off north-westwards beside the Banvie Burn, or Banbhhaidh, sucking pig burn. This track climbs gently through dense natural woods of birch, larch and pine, keeping in sight of the burn which passes through a series of cascades, pools and deep-set ravines, all darkly shaded in bottle green. After a short time, the Rumbling Bridge is reached, a 1762 stone hump-back, which bears witness to the fact that the Banvie Burn, in times of spate, can be so vociferous that it actually "rumbles" the stones and rocks in its bed. Comyn's Road doesn't cross this bridge, which is worthy of admiration for its antiquity, but continues through a gate into the Whim Plantation, which is marked on the O.S. 1:50,000 map. I continued through the woods, enjoying the singing of blackbirds, chaffinches and thrushes, and managed to get myself into a bit of a tizzy looking for a woodpecker which I could distinctly hear rat-a-tatting, but couldn't see. A locked gate marked the end of the plantation, involving a scramble over some rocks at the side of it, and the track then splits again. Comyn's Road stretches straight on, while another path, the beginnings of the Minigaig route, drops down to the burnside where it crosses over the Quarry Bridge, built eight years after the Rumbling Bridge from stones taken from the quarry a few hundred yards upstream. Comyn's Road and the Minigaig, now split, meander on their own separate ways, until they meet up again in Glen Tromie, about 20 miles distant.

Clear of the trees, the landscape changes dramatically. The track stretches clearly up Glen Banvie on the west side of the burn, boldly picking its way over the empty moorland, the brown and green bareness flecked with the white and greys of grazing sheep. The melody of the forest birds is now replaced by the sad dirge of the curlew and the crazy trumpeting of peewits, and the occasional rheumaticky bleat of the gnarled old hill sheep. One scrawny old ewe stood defiantly in the middle of the path, wheezing a growl almost like a dog, until, her temerity forsaken, she trundled off down the bank with a shake of her ancient head. To add to the emptiness of the place, the remains of old dwellings dot the river bank, piles of rubble marking the spots where children once played and men and women lived a hard life. A series of zigzags on the hillside opposite indicate an old path once used by peat cutters fetching their turf from Tom nan Cruach, the Hillock of Peat Stacks. Peat for the castle fires would have been cut here, and stacked up in piles to dry out in the sun and wind, before being carried, probably by pony, down to the castle to heat up the great halls and bedchambers.

The track continues to rise gently, through a pine wood which shows signs of the over-grazing of sheep and red deer which roam these hills. Great herds of red deer stags inhabit Glen Banvie and the vegetation in the glens has been grazed almost flat by their winter feeding. The estate track continues through this pine wood, before tightly bending southwards, but Comyn's Road leaves the track, on a newly bulldozed road, and heads north-west downhill into Glen Bruar, past the old shieling of Ruichlachrie. The house is in good condition, still roofed, though the last tenant left in 1939 to go off and fight in the war. Sadly, he never returned, and the house today offers shelter to only the sheep. This was evidently a populous place at one time, as the ruins and rubble of old buildings testify. I counted the remains of at least nine other buildings, and several enclosures surrounded by the ubiquitous drystone dyke. It's a short distance from here to the Bruar, and the river is easily forded to the house of Cuilltemhuc, another uninhabited shieling.

Several miles downstream of here, at Bruar on the A9, the pretty Falls of Bruar attract passing motorists and picnickers.

The waterfalls cascade through a rocky defile into foaming pools, and the heavily wooded surroundings offer a pleasant spot at which to recover from the busy traffic for an hour or so. But it wasn't always so attractive. Robert Burns, on a visit to Atholl in 1787, mildly chided the then Duke of Atholl in a poem, the "Humble Petition of Bruar Water", because at that time, only bare moorland surrounded the falls.

> Wad then my noble master please,
> To grant my highest wishes,
> He'd shade my banks wi' towering trees,
> and bonnie spreading bushes.

The verses had the desired effect, and the poor ploughman poet, armed with only the simplicity of verse, motivated the rich and powerful Duke of Atholl into planting a vast wood around the waterfalls.

An embankment by the track at Cuilltemhuc gave me some shelter for lunch. The wind was blowing gustily, and there was a spit of rain in the air. As I made my brew, I remembered the old Atholl story of the laughing man of Cuilltemhuc, who, a hundred years ago, was found blind drunk in a water trough laughing his head off. No one ever found out the reason for his mirth, and he died, it is claimed, convulsed in a hearty fit of glee. I couldn't think of a better way to go, although he might have had the decency to share his joke before he succumbed!

An easy-angled heather slope runs in a north-westerly direction away from the river, but the centuries have taken their toll on the tracings of Comyn's Road hereabouts, so it is a question of simply picking a way through the peat hags, the boggy areas and the heather over the hillside to the bothy at Clunes, where a bulldozed track picks up Comyn's Road again. The sky was looking decidedly murky behind me by now, and the pine woods which I had walked through earlier had vanished from sight in a distant shower of rain. I pushed on up and over the low ridge, and in doing so, walked off O.S. Sheet 43.

As I battered on, head down, and eyes fixed firmly on the ground immediately in front of me, I almost walked into the thick of a huge herd of red deer stags. I don't know who got the bigger surprise! Almost as one, they jerked their heads up, turned with a grunt, and loped off pell-mell, hundreds of hooves thudding on the bare ground. They vanished almost immediately into the murk which was quickly enveloping us, leaving behind that pungent deer smell, and a memory of co-ordinated movement and grace. I reached the bothy in the nick of time, for as I was pushing the door open, someone finally switched the light off, and the rain came sheeting down. Clunes (pronounced Cloonis) bothy is not well known, or greatly used, as very few people tend to "stravaig these airts", but I was extremely glad of its shelter. I sat by the streaming window watching the path outside become deeper and deeper in water. Nothing for it but to wait until it eased off. It was only 2.30 p.m., much too early to contemplate settling in for the night, so I made the most of the situation and boiled another brew while I wrote some notes and read a book for a while, until, after about an hour, the rain eased sufficiently to allow me to continue. With the sky about half a shade brighter than it had been before, I stepped tentatively outside, huddled up in the protection of my waterproofs. The dejected whee-whee-whee of a plover sounded as melancholy as the scene around me. What had been bare hillsides an hour earlier, were now snaked in wriggling lines of tiny streams, and the track, winding its way over the low ridge to the north-west, was aflow with dull yellow mud. I couldn't help but think of the clansmen of old, clad in plaids and deerskin brogans, splashing through conditions like this. I wondered what they would have made of my modern waterproofs, gaiters, and vibram-soled boots. We certainly have it easy nowadays. It is ironic that in our search for escapism we rely so much on the super technology of the environment we are trying to escape from.

Evidence of Comyn's Road has been obliterated here, by the crudely built land rover track that I was now splashing through; designed presumably, to take stalkers and their clients further up the glen. Grouse butts dot the hillside, an area to avoid in late August, September and October. Over the crest of the low ridge, the track drops down to run parallel with the waters of the Allt a'Chireachain, where it is joined by the faster flowing Allt a'Baidh. I left the track, and scrambled down the slippery grassy slopes to the confluence of the streams, where a rubble of rocks and boulders made rudimentary stepping stones across to the northern bank.

The remains of several shielings, the Kirrichans, are still clearly visible here. The *Statistical Account* of 1792 describes a shieling in Atholl, thus: "Lower down is heath, peat bog, valleys full of pretty good pasture, and here and there a green spot, with huts on it, to which the women, children and herds retire with the cattle for the summer season." The Kirrichans is indeed a green spot, and I stopped for a few minutes now that the rain had finally stopped. To the north, the long ridge of Sron a'Chleirich, the Nose of the Priest, rose gradually, and it was over this ridge, at 2600 feet, that Comyn's Road had its course.

Several notable expeditions have made their way over the Road in the centuries of its history. In 1295, King Edward I invaded Scotland at the head of an immense army of some 30,000 foot soldiers and 5,000 heavily armed cavalry. Large forces were sent north to survey the country of Badenoch and, as the Earl of Atholl and Sir John Comyn were serving Edward at the time, it seems highly likely that they guided the advance party over the newly built road. In 1644, James Graham, the Marquis of Montrose, returned to Scotland determined to deliver his country from the hands of the three Scottish magnates, Hamilton, Huntly and Argyll. Chased by an army led by Campbell of Argyll, he withdrew his mainly Highland army into Badenoch, using Comyn's Road.

The clatter of steel and the heavy trundling of cannon was a far cry from the peace and solitude of today, as I made my way over the wet and boggy ground to gain the ridge to Sron a'Chleirich. The path can't be traced over this stretch, but it is shown on the O.S. 1:50,000 map from just below the summit of the Sron. Just as I reached the brow of the shoulder, I was overtaken by low cloud which had crept up from the south west; but not before I fixed my position by taking a bearing on the obvious knoll of Meall na Maoile in the south west. With my position fixed on the slope, I took another bearing directly to the trig point on the summit of Sron a'Chleirich. I followed the direction of the compass needle, over short turf and heather, and after about 20 minutes, the trig point loomed up through the mist, spot on target. It was very murky now, and I tried in vain to find the track which is marked on the map. Rather than waste any time, and feeling a bit cocky after successfully finding the trig point, I took a straight bearing to where the track was supposed to meet the county boundary on Bac na Creige, the Bank of the Rocky Hill. Alas, this proved to be a big mistake, as my straight bearing led me across some vile peat hags and evil bogs, with only the speckle of white bog cotton to break the monotony of black mud and glaur. In the dense mist, it made for miserable walking. Still, I looked upon it as a sound exercise in navigation, and after crossing, and recognizing, the headwaters of the Feithe nan Mad, climbing the steeper slopes of Bac na Creige to the plateau, I found rusted old fence post which indicated the boundary between Atholl and Badenoch; but still no path. Even so I didn't worry unduly, as all I really had to do was continue in a due north direction, and I was bound, eventually, to come across the slopes which lead down to the Allt Gharbh Gaig, which runs into Gaick. As it happened, the cloud lifted, to find me on the broad featureless plateau of Bac na Creige. I made my way carefully to the north-west slopes of the hill, where I came across the path, running diagonally across the steep slopes.

The antiquity of this track can be seen here, as it runs along an actual shelf cut into the steep hillside, a shelf which appears to be too well defined and constant, to be natural.

Picking my way down the track, I enjoyed the transformation of the landscape below me. The change, from barren monotonous plateau to steep-sided rocky glen, with broken crags and foaming burns, is sudden and dramatic. The hillside opposite, Meall Odhar Aillig, was spouting a myriad of white waterfalls, some tumultuous and roaring, some mere dribbles, and below, the river roared its way down in the narrow defile. A good footbridge crosses the Allt Gharbh Gaig, a metal affair, overlaid with turf. I crossed it, then stopped to photograph the vivid greens and browns of the wild hillside, the thrashing waters of the river, and the black crags which rose high all around. It was a scene of rousing splendour, and such a contrast to the emptiness of the plateau above. The track carried me down the glen, running alongside the river, until we reached the alluvial flats of Gaick. Red deer virtually coated the hillsides, the young ones bleating madly and the hinds snorting their annoyance as they tried to graze in peace. A family of young dippers, water ouzels, spurted ahead of me trying like mad to imitate their swerving parents, and a wheatear chuckled noisily from a rock beside the path. I drank in the wildness as I looked for a campsite beside the river, finding it hard to believe that this area, Gaick, through the ages, was ever supposed to be the haunt of the occult and all things supernatural. Many are the tales of misdeed and misfortune in the steep confines of this glen, and a Gaelic bard of the eighteenth century once penned these words of warning: "Black Gaick of the wind whistling crooked glens, ever enticing her admirers to their destruction." Seton Gordon, in his *Highways and Byways in the Central Highlands*, tells the story of the Fairy Sweetheart, the Leannan Sith, who had her home in the hills of Gaick. She had the habit of appearing before hunters in the forest, who were so entranced by her great beauty that they immediately fell in love with her. Sadly, it was believed that the earthly wives of those who fell for the fairy were then in great danger of being hurt by their supernatural rival. For centuries, Gaick stalkers have reported sightings of tiny women dressed in green, doll-like creatures who, in the lonely confines of the higher corries, follow the herds of red deer and milk the hinds like cattle. The fairy folk of course have repeatedly been seen all over the Highlands, not just in Gaick. As recently as 1958, Colonel Jimmy Dennis, while out stalking in the Gaick Hills spotted something moving near a stream. He looked through his telescope for a better look, but saw nothing. However, by shading his eyes from the glare of the sun, he could just discern the shape of a tiny human creature, dressed like a child in a siren suit and pixie hood. He approached the spot as quickly as he could, but couldn't find any trace of the mysterious figure at all. Several years later, he told his story to an old retired stalker from a neighbouring forest. The old man looked at him queerly, pulled his pipe from his mouth and said, "Then ye've seen the spite o'Gaick."

The Comyn's link with the evil forces which allegedly occur in Gaick could well have been forged in the late fourteenth century, when Walter Comyn of Ruthven, in a mood of cruel sensuousness, decreed that all the women of Badenoch between the ages of twelve and thirty should work in the fields stark naked. He went through the hill country to Atholl and the day of this return was fixed for the infamous exhibition. He never did return, although his horse did; terrified and foaming at the mouth, and trailing in one of the stirrups the torn-off leg of the Comyn! A search was instantly made, and at a place called Leum na Feinne in Gaick, the remains of the body were discovered, with two gorged eagles preying gluttonously on it. Comyn's gory end was attributed to witchcraft, and the two eagles were reckoned to be the supernatural forms of two of the mothers of the harvest girls. A centuries-old Badenoch curse, "Diol Bhaltair an Gaig ort", Walter's fate in Gaick on you, recalls the old story.

I lay in my little tent by the chattering river, and considered these tales of fairies and witches. Lapwings, plummeting around' in the dusk, made hooting noises, and oystercatchers vociferously squeaked their aggression at some obscure annoyance. The occasional cough or grunt of a deer floated in the still night air, and the rumble and continuous chatter of the river could so easily, at times, sound like the drone of distant voices. In the solitude and seclusion of a Highland glen, especially when it is almost dark and one can't see everything one hears, one's mind becomes receptive to the slightest hint of the unknown, and the atmosphere created by this perception has the faculty of implanting a suggestion of alarm, or even fear, to such an extent, that a fertile imagination could quite easily be stimulated. I certainly would not admit to believing in the little people, or the supernatural, but by the same token, nor do I disbelieve. To me, the tales and legends of old add a colour and romance to these areas which have the necessary combination of history and atmosphere to sustain them, and to appreciate that atmosphere to the full, one must keep an open mind on such things. The folklore of old is a powerful motivation to experience the winds and whispers of our former homeland, and the person who seeks these perceptions can enjoy a fulfilment which is one of the great rewards of the outdoors.

I was still turning these thoughts over in my mind as I packed up in the morning. A gloomy sky hung over the flat strath of Gaick, and the shooting lodge stood lonely and remote at the head of Loch an t-Seilich. There wasn't a hint of habitation, the tenants probably arrive later in the summer to stay through to the deer stalking season. On all sides of this flat strath, the hills rise to over 2000 feet, steep sided and smooth, perfect examples of potential avalanche slopes; and they are just that. Drifting clouds of snow blow across the flat plateaux during the winter, and pile up in the lee side of the slope, in great depths, just waiting for someone, or something, to trigger them off into thundering white cascades of sliding rolling snow. It was probably an avalanche which caused one of Gaick's best-known "supernatural" happenings. In January of 1800, Black John MacPherson of Ballachroan took four companions on a shooting expedition to Gaick. The weather was ferocious, with strong winds and drifting snow, but he ridiculed the warnings of his friends who told him he was crazy going off in such weather. The nights were spent in a hut near to where the present lodge is situated, and one night, a bright fire was spotted burning high on the summit of the hill above them. They investigated, but no trace of the fire was found on the snowy slope. This was taken as a bad omen, and again, Black John was advised to quit the expedition, and go home. He disagreed, saying that he must stay on. Several days later, the hut was found to be destroyed, torn to shreds and devastated almost beyond recognition by some powerful, malevolent force. Black John and the companions who stayed with him were all found dead in the vicinity. The annihilation, so sudden and complete, was put down to supernatural causes, although it is now generally believed that a huge avalanche was the power which destroyed the hut and its unfortunate residents. No one, though, has yet put forward a theory to explain the mysterious fire.

An estate track runs down the length of the east bank of Loch an t-Seilich to Glen Tromie, but, according to the historians, Comyn's Road took the more direct route along the west bank, before rising over the shoulder of Bogha-Cloiche, to descend into Glen Tromie down the long heathery slopes of Maol an t-Seilich. It looks a fearful route on the map, as the steep slopes of Bogha-Cloiche appear to fall directly into the waters of the loch, but, in reality, a pony track runs across the slopes starting from the footbridge over the river directly west of Gaick Lodge. It proved to be a very pleasant walk, along the narrow track with ever-widening views of the loch and the broad glen at its head. Loch an t-Seilich is dammed at its northern end, as part of one of Scotland's very first hydro-electric schemes, built in 1940. From the loch, a five-mile tunnel burrows below the mountains to Loch Cuaich in the west, and then west to Dalwhinnie and by an aqueduct to Loch Ericht.

The path climbs quickly above the loch, over the broad shoulder and then down the long gentle slopes to the glen. An old Gaelic bard once described Glen Tromie as "Gleann Tromaidh nan Siantan", the glen of the stormy blasts, and in the depths of winter, when the bare birches are cold and grey against the snow-covered ground, and the sky above has that heavy menace of winter storm, then that statement just about sums it up, but in spring, summer and autumn, it is a different place entirely. The banks of the River Tromie are decorated with natural birch, alder and juniper, the slopes on either side are gentle, and there is a calmness and tranquillity which you cannot find on the rest of Comyn's Road, however grand it may be. Across the river is Bhran Cottage, uninhabited and usually locked up. I didn't cross the river to the estate path, but stayed on the west bank where the track passes some more signs of past settlements, before making its way up the long ascent of Sron na Gaoithe, the Nose of the Winds, then finally making its last descent to Ruthven.

As I climbed out of the glen, I noticed a prominent cairn, marked on the map as Carn Pheigith, Peggy's Cairn. Tradition has it that this mound of stones marks the burial place of one Peggy, a suicide of the fourteenth century. Before it became fashionable to deface our mountains with cairns, heaps of stones were erected over the graves of the dead, to secure them from wolves. It became customary to toss another stone on top as you passed by, hence the proverb, "Were I dead, you would not throw a stone on it", meaning, you don't have much friendship for me.

It was a gentle climb over the Sron, and as I passed the crest of the ridge, the views opened up before me to the north. Newtonmore and Kingussie nestled under the great rounded swell of the Monadhliath Mountains, and here and there a tell-tale splash of silver showed where the River Spey meandered through this, the flattest stretch of its otherwise volatile course from its source high in the hills of Corrieyairack, to its mouth in the North Sea. The track can easily be seen from here, picking its way over the mild heather slopes towards the small crest of Beinn Bhuidhe, a delightful finish to the walk. With extensive views to the north and west, it was only a matter of time before the round high tops of the Cairngorms came into sight in the east, and sure enough, there they were, Carn Ban Mor and the Glen Feshie tops, still wreathed in the remnants of the winter snow. I flushed several grouse from the heather, their "go-back go-back" warnings having little effect on me now that I was almost home. A cuckoo droned on from somewhere down below, that lazy bird which in these parts of Speyside, tend to parasitize the nests of meadow pipits, the commonest bird on these high moors.

Here and there, there were patches of bog myrtle interspersed with the heather, scenting the air with that musty, minty scent. White patches of chickweed wintergreen, mountain everlasting, and fir clubmoss broke up the prevalent greenery, and it wasn't long before I was treading over short-cropped turf, with sandy embankments alive with rabbits, the heather slopes having given way to grassy braes. A couple of gates took me past more old ruins, before the biggest ruin of them all came into view, the gaunt fire-destroyed walls of Ruthven Barracks. General Wade reconstructed the building for his dragoons on the prehistoric mound which Comyn had also used in the thirteenth century, but it was only to stand for a matter of some twenty-five years, before being burnt down in 1746 on the orders of Bonnie Prince Charlie on the run from Culloden.

It is only a mile and a half or so to Kingussie, by the road below the interminable roarings of the new A9 dual carriageway, the latest, and without doubt, the least attractive of all the roads through the Grampians.

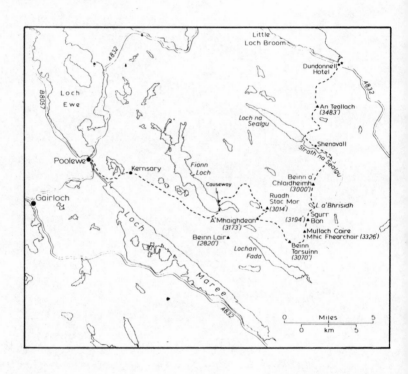

ROUTE 9: DUNDONNELL TO POOLEWE: OVER THE GREAT WILDERNESS

A 30-mile, 2-camp, high-level mountain walk, taking in 8 Munros. This is a difficult walk over very remote terrain and should only be attempted by experienced mountain backpackers.
   Map required: O.S. 1:50,000, Sheet 19.

Leave Dundonnell Hotel and walk E. on A832 for ½ mile. Strike S. on path climbing quickly up ridge of Meall Garbh and on to high plateau N.W. of Glas Mheall Mor, 2 miles. Walk S. for ½ mile to edge of corrie N. of Bidean a Ghlas Thuill and climb S. to the summit of An Teallach, 3483 feet. Descend S.W. to bealach and climb Sgurr Fiona, 3474 feet (newly promoted Munro). Follow ridge over Lord Berkeley's Seat, and the Corrag Bhuidhe Buttress. A track misses the difficulties by running alongside on the S.W. Ascend Sail Liath, and descend S.E. slopes to Shenavall path. Camp or bothy at Shenavall. Follow Abhainn Strath na Sealga S.W. for almost a mile, ford the river and climb N.E. slopes of Beinn a'Chlaidheimh, 3000 feet, 1 mile. Follow ridge S., skirting above E. side of Loch a'Bhrisidh, and ascend slopes of Sgurr Ban, 3194 feet, 2¼ miles. Descend S. slopes of Sgurr Ban and climb steep slopes of Mullach Coire Mhic Fhearchair, 3326 feet. Descend S., skirting N.W. slopes of Meall Garbh on footpath, and climb to summit of Beinn Tarsuinn, 3000 feet, 2 miles. Take care on the narrow ridge of Tarsuinn, and walk W., then N.W., dropping down W. before the end of the ridge, to the bealach to S.E. of Stac a'Chaorruinn. Climb easy slopes of A'Mhaighdean, and camp on bealach between A'Mhaighdean and Ruadh Stac Mor. Ascend A'Mhaighdean, 3173 feet and Rhuadh Stac Mor, 3014 feet, from camp. Follow path on N. side of Fuar Loch Mor in a N.W. direction until it meets the Gleann na Muice Beag path, 2 miles. Follow path

S.W. and W. to Carnmore, 1¾ miles, S. over causeway between Dubh Loch and Fionn Loch and then W.N.W. below steep slopes of Meal Mheinnidh and Beinn Airigh Charr to Kernsary, 8 miles. From Kernsary take footpath on N. shore of Loch Kernsary for 3 miles to Poolewe.

Between the long arms of Loch Maree and Little Loch Broom in Wester Ross, there lies a great tangle of wild mountain and high lonely lochans. These days the word "wilderness" is greatly overused and misapplied, but for the vast deer forests of Strathnashealag, Fisherfield and Letterewe, "wilderness" is an apt description.

No bulldozed tracks cast vile scars on this landscape; no signposts simplify route-finding, and cairns are restricted to the very summits of the mountains; buildings are confined to a mere scattered handful of bothies or shooting huts, and the area is jealously guarded by landowners who tend to discourage visitors. Their task, mind you, is not a difficult one, as the natural barriers of roughness and vast distances preclude all but the most experienced and enthusiastic walkers and climbers. It may seem strange, then, that I have decided, after much wrestling with my conscience I confess, to include this walk in a book on backpacking. This is an area priceless in its solitude, where, because of the enormous distances from habitation even a trivial accident could well have serious consequences, an area of mountain so rough and remote that very often scrambling is involved, an area in which in the event of an accident the most serious consequences could follow. It is for these reasons that I have included it. In recent years, the mystery surrounding the "Great Wilderness" has largely evaporated due to various articles and features in mountaineering journals and books. But even armed with route descriptions, the backpacker still has to hump his load over some very rough and wild protuberances, definitely not an area for the first-time visitor to Scotland; not an area for the backpacking tyro; most definitely not an area for the inexperienced or unfit. I must emphasize this. These deer forests are a place to aspire to, an area in which to wander only when the long hill apprenticeship has been served on lesser hills, a climax to all that is best in Scottish backpacking. If you are new to backpacking in Scotland, don't plan to head off for Dundonnell tomorrow; but read on ... and dream ... one day perhaps ...

Jeff Faulkner is a ski instructor in Aviemore, and unlike many of his breed, is a keen mountain man, even when the mountains are bare of snow. An erstwhile fell runner and rock climber, he has long experience of instructing and wandering the Bens, an ideal companion, in fact, for a tramp through the Great Wilderness. We planned a three-day jaunt from the bristles and jagged spires of An Teallach, a monster of a hill just south of Dundonnell at the head of Little Loch Broom, over the broad and fertile Strath na Sealga, to Beinn a'Chlaidheimh, Sgurr Ban, Mullach Coire Mhic Fhearchair, Beinn Tarsuinn, A'Mhaighdean (said to be the most inaccessible hill in Scotland), Ruadh Stac Mor, and then by way of Carnmore and Fionn Loch to Poolewe, a total distance of some 30 rough miles, taking in eight remote Munros, and involving over 11,500 feet of climbing.

Leaving my car by the post office in Poolewe, we caught the 8.20 a.m. bus to Dundonnell, an hour-long journey zigzagging through the scattered croftships and villages which dot this indented coastline. We shared the bus with another couple, a boy and girl, who were also planning to walk from Dundonnell to Poolewe, although their trip was not quite as ambitious as ours. They intended walking from Dundonnell House, via Corrie Hallie, through Gleann na Muice to the Fionn Loch, where he intended spending a few days trout fishing, while she, not to be cast as a "fishing widow", would climb some of the surrounding hills. Jeff wished him luck with the fishing. "I've got to catch them," he replied. "The alternative doesn't bear thinking about – dehydrated mince, ugh!" We parted company outside the Dundonnell Hotel; they to walk the couple of miles up the road to Corrie Hallie, while Jeff and I struck southwards off the road, to take the track to An Teallach which begins opposite the climbers' hut known as the Smiddy.

The sun was shining and it was hot as we climbed the lower slopes. The first thousand feet or so of An Teallach are steep, but a good path, if a little on the muddy side, makes walking easy. As we climbed, we looked back from time to time to admire the view which was gradually unfolding behind us. Across Little Loch Broom, the twin-peaked Beinn Ghobhlach rose, dark and well shaped, with the long black outline of the Coigach Hills peeping over its shoulder. Beyond Coigach, we had a tantalizing glimpse of the far north and the great hills of Sutherland. Out to sea the sky was dark and ominous, and it looked as though the weather was shortly to close in on us, not ideal conditions for this particular ploy. An Teallach is more of a small range of peaks than one single mountain, and to traverse its bristling crest, over a multitude of pinnacles and spires, requires a fair amount of scrambling and a steady head. For experienced walkers and climbers An Teallach presents no more than an exciting ridge scramble, but with thirty-pound rucksacks strapped around our shoulders, it looked as though our traverse could be a memorable one. The worst (or best) of the pinnacles can all be bypassed by a narrow path on the south-west side of the ridge, but Jeff, being a keen rock man, insisted on us at least trying to go over the tops. It was with good foresight that he brought along a 90-foot, 9-millimetre climbing rope!

The Ordnance Survey map, Sheet 19, Gairloch and Ullapool, indicates a path running up the crest of a ridge to the higher northern slopes of An Teallach. For some reason, we missed this particular path, but were caught up in another, an excellent one, up the long green Coire a Mhuillin immediately below the steep slopes of An Teallach's northern quartz-capped peak, Glas Mheall Mor. This path took us all the way to the bealach between an unnamed top and the actual summit slopes of An Teallach, Bidean a Ghlas Thuill, 3483 feet. As we had feared, the mists began to envelop us as we climbed the steep and rocky slopes to the summit. An Teallach means The Forge, from the smoke-like clouds which habitually curl around its eleven tops. It was certainly living up to its name now.

We didn't linger by the trig point summit, but followed the ridge downwards towards the high bealach before Sgurr Fiona, the Peak of Wine. From this bealach vantage point, the dark waters of Loch Toll an Lochain could be seen lapping far below us. This lochan, and the sandstone-tiered cliffs which rise from its banks, offer arguably the finest corrie architecture in all of Scotland, vying with the magnificent Coire Mhic Fhearchair of Beinn Eighe in Torridon. From the corrie below it's a superb sight, the cliffs rising apparently sheer from a skirt of red scree, tier upon tier of red sandstone, reaching the sky in a jagged outline of pinnacles and peaks, and even from our high bealach it should have been an inspiring, daunting sight, but the eternal cloud round The Forge well and truly blocked the view, and made our task that little bit more tricky.

Back into the clouds we climbed, on and up to the jagged summit of Sgurr Fiona. From here we felt, rather than saw, the steepness of the ground around us, and our disappointment at not catching a view of the line of ridge before us was soon replaced by an all-consuming excitement as the crazy overhanging pinnacle of Lord Berkeley's Seat came into view through the mist. Jeff began climbing as I fumbled for my camera, but a shout of excitement soon had me clambering up the sandstone blocks beside him. It was as though we stood on the edge of nothing. Below our feet, only air and mist separated us from a plunging slab well over 100 feet below. The slab continued to plunge for over a thousand feet into Loch Toll an Lochain. I felt uneasy as I stood on the tilting pinnacle, and it was with a vague relief that I followed Jeff along the tight sandstone crest. Up and down we went, over the four Corrag Bhuidhe pinnacles, narrow and exposed, but easy enough if we used hands as well as feet, superb ridge walking. One or two of the descents were a little tricky as our bulky rucksacks either jammed in the narrow gullies, or tried to push us outwards as we negotiated the awkward sections, but we trod delicately, like Agag, if a little slowly. The next peak was the one we feared: the Corrag Bhuidhe Buttress. This exposed pinnacle was reputed to have a "Bad Step" on its descent, the scene of a couple of fatalities in the early 1970s. Jeff was quietly confident, insisting that at least we take a look at it, so we stayed with the crest of the ridge, with me making sure that at all times the easy path which skirts the pinnacles was well within view. We clambered over the summit boulders, delighting in its apparent ease, when suddenly, the ground just dropped away in front of us. The vague path, of worn pink sandstone, just seemed to disappear over the edge. We had reached the Bad Step. Jeff took a closer look, edging delicately down the slimy-looking chimney. "It'll go all right," he shouted, climbing back up, "but not with these bloody packs on. We'll have to lower them down on the rope." I edged my way down, on wet sloping footholds, but with good confidence-boosting handholds. The move consisted of a downwards step, a slight traverse to the right on a narrow ledge, then careful edging down a steep wet corner. The packs followed me down, one at a time, tied to the rope. Soon Jeff was tiptoeing down beside me out of the mist, thoroughly delighted to be on steep ground, relishing the exposure and steepness of the place. We made our way down another steepish pitch in the same way, before dropping down easier slopes to the Cadha Ghobhlach, a broad bealach with indented steep gullies dropping down into the murk below. We felt rather pleased with ourselves. Our antics were hardly backpacking, but it was a good feeling to have traversed the split and riven skyline of this fine mountain. We decided that we deserved a late lunch.

The last peak of the traverse now lay before us, its top just clear of the steadily rising cloud. Sail Liath, the Grey Heel, was simply an easy walk up bouldery slopes, a bit of an afterthought following the excitement of Corrag Bhuidhe, and we merrily made our way down the steep and craggy slopes towards the green valley of Strath na Sealga. As we descended, the cloud level rose, and across the wide strath, the trident-topped Beinn Dearg Mhor gradually shrugged off its cloak of cloud to reveal a magnificent mountain, for all the world like a smaller version of An Teallach. Below its steep slopes, Loch na Sealga, fed by some of the remotest mountain streams in Scotland, stretched in a north-western slant towards the lovely Gruinard Bay, the lapping waters and shingle beach tempting us to take a slight diversion for a bathe. There is something totally delightful and primitive about working up a lather of sweat, leaping down a mountain slope, before stripping off and plunging into the cool waters of a loch. The icy cold had us gasping and spluttering, before a cloud of horseflies, the dreaded clegs, chased us back into our clothes again.

Strath na Sealga, or more correctly Sheallag, is the "Valley of Hunting". It is a delightful place, cradling the meandering Abhainn Strath na Sealga, the hills on either side a deep purple brown, with cattle grazing on the lower slopes. Spotted orchids and bog asphodel, lousewort and milkwort, add fringes of colour to the green valley floor, all made fragrant by the rich aromatic leaves of the plentiful bog myrtle. Curlews warbled, a redstart stood rasping away on a rock, and down the loch a bit, some bird went splashing into the glittering waters, possibly a diver. Our traverse, descent and swim had shrugged off the remnants of our normal life; we were now in, and felt part of, this great wilderness which lay around us.

Shenavall Bothy is situated about a mile south-east of the head of the loch; once housing a deer watcher, it has been untenanted for many a year, apart from the walkers and climbers who use the building, outwith the shooting season only, with the estate's blessing. We pitched our tent a little way off from the bothy, preferring the scent of a westerly breeze whispering through the open tent door to the stuffy, damp smell of the bothy. We ate the evening away; soup, *risotto*, prawn Provencal, and coffee, all freeze dried but five-star stuff nevertheless. To add a touch of luxuriant bliss, we lay outside in the warm evening and watched a magnificent sunset over the waters of the loch, contentedly sipping drams of Drambuie! And people often ask what fun there is to be had "roughing it"!

As the evening lengthened, the dying sun cast a warm glow over Beinn Dearg Mhor and its easterly neighbour, Beinn a'Chlaidheimh, the Hill of the Swords. This hill was our starter for the morning, and we were up, breakfasted and away by 7 a.m., the early start being attributed to more than pure enthusiasm. A herd of cattle decided to have a bellowing match across our tent during the wee sma' hours, and an inquisitive calf continually thrust its wet and slobbery nose through the open tent door.

Beinn a'Chlaidheimh, or Beinn a Clay, lies due south of the bothy, the summit being about two miles as the crow flies, although crows don't have to negotiate the often hazardous Sealga River. The northern slopes of the hill looked very steep and craggy, so we diverted eastwards along the riverbank to attack the slopes where they looked less inhospitable. As luck would have it, we managed to cross the river dryshod, leaping from stone to stone with more brashness than agility. The steep heathery slopes made difficult going; we swore and sweated our way upwards through the clagging ling heather and assorted heaths, slipping on the wet muddy undergrowth and wishing we had something solid to walk on. A long narrow gully a little to our right beckoned invitingly. It looked cool in there, and although it seemed to steepen near the top, we did have a rope with us. We decided it would make an interesting detour. We climbed and clambered below waterfalls, over slippy moss-covered rocks and admired the gardens of alpines growing luxuriantly on the wet rock ledges. In the confines of the gully, protected from the grazings of deer and sheep, yellow globe-flowers grew in abundance, with mountain avens, heath violet, wood anemone, mountain sorrel, and great adornments of starry saxifrage.

Marvellous as the plants may have been, our gully was a dead end. We made one or two attempts at climbing out on the greasy rock, and after passing the smelly remains of a red deer, decided that prudence was the best course in the circumstances. We retraced our way back on to the heather, put the bit between our teeth, and struggled on. As we climbed higher, the heather gave way to alpine grasses, and then great fields of white quartzite which cap the summits of many of the surrounding hills. The summit ridge of Beinn a'Chlaidheimh, which sits spot on the Munro plimsoll line of 3000 feet, is tent like, tight and narrow, a good ridge over three separate tops. From the summit the view showed us wilderness a plenty in all directions. Below, Loch a'Bhrisidh was set in a craggy cirque, before a dazzling white slope of quartzite stretched up to the summit of Sgurr Ban, appropriately enough, the White Peak. Across the broad gulf of Gleann na Muice to the west, the long craggy gneiss-outcropped slopes of Ruadh Stac Mor and A'Mhaighdean rose into a broiling turmoil of cloud, defending to the last their proud reputations as Scotland's remotest Munros. To the north, An Teallach, The Forge, had doused its smoky fires, and stood clear in a culmination of slashed peaks and pinnacles, allowing us to glimpse over its shoulder to the far north.

Sgurr Ban, although splendidly quartz capped, can be ascended on grass for much of its 1000-foot climb from the bealach. As we moved upwards, we disturbed a roost of ptarmigan chicks, the mother running around in circles dragging a wing, an old ploy to try and tempt us away from her brood. The youngsters were hilarious; little balls of fluff running downhill so fast that they continually fell head over heels, rolling down the slope as much as they ran, like tiny furry Easter eggs.

Sgurr Ban has a broad plateau summit, almost like a Cairngorm top, but immediately south, Mullach Coire Mhic Fhearchair, our next Munro, presented a contrasting image. Steep, bouldery, its slopes riven and seamed with long scree gullies and protruding crags running upwards to its narrow top. We brewed up by a tiny lochan at its foot and enjoyed some cheese and Mars Bars before promptly falling asleep. So much for the modern dynamic backpacker. The chill of sweat-dampened clothes woke us and we shivered; we had dozed off for about three-quarters of an hour, although it seemed as though we had just closed our eyes for a moment. Refreshed, we wound our way up Mullach's slopes, three steps up, two back, on the steep loose scree. The top is a fine one, with a large cairn indicating the 3326 feet above sea level, the highest summit of the round. The western face of the hill is of pink sandstone, split by great searing gullies. The summit cone, like Sgurr Ban, is of Cambrian quartzite, white and dazzling in the sun, greasy and foul in the rain. The main feature of Mullach is a mile-long ridge of gneiss which extends south-eastwards into the head of Gleann an Nid, terminating in a series if spiring pinnacles.

Between us and our next Munro, Beinn Tarsuinn was a little bump top, Meall Garbh. Lying as it does at the corner of the curving ridge, it can be easily avoided by following a very good path which runs along the foot of its north-west-facing slopes, a patch which was alive with jumping high-altitude frogs. A boggy bealach leads on to the grassy slopes of Tarsuinn. This mountain forms the red-sandstone-tiered headwall of Gleann na Muice, and forms a marvellous curving ridge cradling a high lochan in its clench. From the summit the views northwards down the glen are quite dramatic; a long broadening valley reaching far down to the slopes of An Teallach. The ridge we had just walked forms a mighty barrier to the east, and to the north-west, the tops of A'Mhaighdean and Ruadh Stac Mor had at long last cast off their cloudy cap, showing a deep gneiss-splattered bealach between them. Southwards, the great bulk of Slioch rose high over the dark waters of Lochan Fada, and beyond, the sharp magnificence of the Torridon Hills. This was the first time I have ever stood on a Scottish mountain top without seeing signs of man. Not a track, not a road, not one blemish; nothing but fold upon fold of mountain, vast, rolling and pinnacled as far as the eye could see. It was a stunning thought that in the event of an accident, it would take a day's walking in any direction to reach help, with possibly another day for help to come back in. A long time indeed to lie with a broken leg!

This sobering thought made us extra careful on the narrow sandstone crest of Tarsuinn's ridge. A short drop from the summit takes you on to a broad flat-topped table, then a series of pinnacles, weathered and seamed, which call for some careful scrambling. We had heard somewhere of a Bad Step on this ridge, but even assiduously following the skyline, we didn't come across anything too nasty. It could well be a different story in mist and rain though!

Dropping off the ridge before its end, we loped down steep scree slopes to the broad peat-hag riven bealach below. Time for another brew. I have found from bitter experience that the only way to carry a heavy rucksack over mountains is to take it easy and slow, with plenty of tea breaks. I have gone through the phase of bashing on, becoming increasingly tired, so that the last hours of the day pass in a haze of sweaty fatigue. That's not fun. The words of the old Irish folk song, "Takin' it easy and takin' it slow", should be the mountain backpacker's motto, and in that way you can enjoy the solitude and peace of a high-level camp, instead of just crashing out as soon as you lay down your sleeping bag.

Hamish Brown had once told me that the view from A'Mhaighdean was the finest in all Scotland; that is, if you are blessed with good weather, which in these parts is the exception rather than the norm. With a hot sun burning our backs it seemed that we were being blessed so we faced the long easy slopes to A'Mhaighdean, this route from the east being the only easy way to climb the mountain, the most inaccessible in the country. From every other direction, A'Mhaighdean appears as a high cliff-girt precipice, although the contours of the O.S. map make it look more benign than it actually is.

In high spirits as we neared the end of our day, we moved on straight uphill, taking one or two smaller gneiss crags in our stride. One in particular took our fancy, although we could easily have walked around it, and I led up a series of stepped rocks, balancing delicately on the rounded footholds, pulling up on good clean "juggies". This sort of thing can be a little on the risky side; a slip could have meant a fall of some fifty feet, but for pure exhilaration and fun it was tremendous. Little jaunts like this make a walking trip memorable; technically very easy but good fun.

Before the final rise to A'Mhaighdean, we cut across north-westwards to the bealach to look for a campsite. It was an ideal spot, a large fold of grey gneiss outcrops and tiny nestling lochans. We found a flat stretch of grass near the edge of the corrie rim, and put the tent up, carefully positioning the door so that we could have a good view from our sleeping bags. And what a view it was. Below us the dark waters of the cliff-circled Fuar Loch Mor were accentuated by the red cliffs and screes of Ruadh Stac Mor, and from its lapping waters a scene of loch-splattered high moorland, green and grey with gneiss outcrops, stretched gauntly and strangely beautiful to the west. In the distance, the Summer Isles floated on a sea of translucent blue, and beyond, the edge of the Atlantic. Jeff organized the camp as I ran around trigger happy with my camera, blasting off a 36-exposure film in almost as many seconds.

With the camp ready, A'Mhaighdean, the Maiden, awaited our attentions. Unencumbered by packs, we felt light and free, and the grassy slopes, although steep, seemed easy enough. A flat grassy plateau greeted us as we romped upwards, and over the rim, a vast watery scene of lochs and sea appeared, stretched out below us in all its glory. Immediately next to us, the great long ramparts of Ben Lair separated us from Loch Maree, the Torridon Hills thrusting up beyond. A jagged outline, which must have been the Cuillin of Skye, peeped over Beinn Eighe's shoulder, and away across the sea, the long ridge of Trotternish seemed to stretch out into the hills of Harris. Remote lochs lay below us; Gorm Loch Mor, the Dubh Loch, and the Fionn Loch stretched seawards to the great spread of

Loch Ewe and the open sea, and on either side of the Fionn Loch, great crags rose skywards, Beinn Airigh Charr and the Carnmore Crags, massive heights of almost overhanging rocks rising from vast slabs. The whole panorama was breathtaking, and my finger grew restless on my camera again. We moved on up to the actual summit, a tiny cairn as warrants the most inaccessible top in Scotland, marking the point 3173 feet above sea level. We sat there for what seemed an age, perched high on this lofty eyrie, drinking in the loch-glittering west. The views from every conceivable angle were splendid and remote, whilst the country closer at hand had that primeval wildness which one can only expect in dreams.

A deep gnawing hunger eventually dragged us away, back down to the tent on our high bealach. A quick brew of tea, laced with some lemon juice, satisfied the thirst and gave a sharp edge to the hunger, which was soon allayed by a mixture of beef and tomato soup, followed by minced beef with tomato and spaghetti, blackcurrant and rice pudding, topped off with Drambuie coffees. We had fully intended climbing Ruadh Stac Mor from camp after supper, but we were so full all we could do was belch and sip a drop of whisky as we watched shreds of cloud pass across a low orange sun on the far horizon. We were soon yawning our way to bed; even the prospect of another sunset couldn't keep us up tonight.

We woke early, the early morning sun making the inside of the tent unbearably hot. We breakfasted outside on *muesli,* cheese and oatcakes, packed up the tent, and moved off a mere couple of hundred yards to dump our packs by a stone howff. The cliffs of Ruadh Stac Mor are steep and broken hereabouts, but the odd grass and scree gully gives easy access to the summit plateau. We quickly climbed up one of these, and within ten minutes of leaving our packs stood beside the summit cairn, a trig point made of local stone rather than the normal white concrete. Although only 8.30, thin wisps of cloud were already threatening to close up the blue sky. To the east, dark clouds were rolling laboriously across the Fannichs, and it felt very warm and muggy; thundery perhaps? We didn't linger; we still had a good 14-mile trek back to Poolewe and we had no idea what the path would be like. An easy scramble wriggled us through the cliffs again, back to the packs, and a superbly built stalkers' path took us quickly off the bealach, below the skirt of red scree which forms the base of the Ruadh Stac Mor cliffs, past the brooding Fuar Loch Mor, and down over the high gneiss-patched moor land to the main Dundonnell to Poolewe track beside Lochan Feith Mhic-Illean.

This track winds its way up from Strath na Sealga by way of Glen na Muice and Gleann na Muice Beag, and continues as a right of way to either Poolewe or, alternatively, Letterewe on Loch Maree by way of the Bealach Mheinnidh, through routes which must be the most magnificent in Scotland. Our early prophesy — too bright by seven, rain by eleven — wasn't one hundred per cent accurate, as although the sky had now clouded over completely, the cloud ceiling was very high and it was still hot. Despite the heat, we pushed on, our spirits high in these wonderful surroundings, as we dropped down the steep slopes towards the lonely house of Carnmore, empty for much of the year but used as a shooting lodge during the season. What a magnificent setting for a house. Situated below the frowning beetling cliffs of Beinn a Chaisgein Mor and Sgurr na Laocainn, the building is well and truly dwarfed to insignificance. The Dubh Loch lies in front, as black as its name, reflecting the graceful crested ridge of A'Mhaighdean as it rises almost sheer from the lonely green corrie at the head of the loch. To the south, the solid vertical wall of Beinn Lair rises to the sky, split only by the high Bealach Mheinnidh as it carried its track over to Loch Mareeside. Down here by the lochside, dippers dashed about hurriedly, meadow pipits cavorted in loud song, and twites twittered. If you are lucky you may hear the sad piping of a golden plover, or see high above you the spiralling flight of an eagle, for these wild crags are a favourite haunt of theirs.

From the narrow stone causeway which separates the

montane Dubh Loch from the more tranquil Fionn Loch (the black loch and the white loch), we gazed back on this primeval sanctuary. It is a place of such utter beauty and grandeur that it would be a grotesque work of vandalism to try and tame it with roads or bulldozed tracks, or any other horror of so-called progress and civilization. Only well-made paths thread this wilderness, and it is almost unbelievable that twice in the past few years, threats of proposed hydro-electric schemes for this area have been made. We, as backpackers and walkers, have a duty to observe and protect wilderness like this, for once the cancer of man has made inroads, the magnificence is lost forever.

Ten long miles now separated us from Poolewe; around the pink pebbled beach of the Fionn Loch, and below the great overhangs of Meall Mheinnidh and Beinn Airigh Charr, both excellent rock-climbing areas, the latter known to rockmen as Martha's Peak. The countryside now begins to flatten out, and the path becomes indistinct, in fact downright boggy. A couple of miles north of here there is an area ominously marked on the map as the Bad Bog. You have been warned. These bogs make up part of a nasty "sting in the tail" to this expedition. We danced our way across from tussock to tussock, a mis-step resulting in gluttonous oozings and sucking gurgles, and eventually emerged, peat splattered, by the stile into the forestry plantation east of Loch Kernsary. We then promptly lost ourselves in the second part of the "sting in the tail". Jeff reckoned the path ran through the middle of the plantation, and I reckoned it followed the stream which had kept us company for the past three or so miles. We tossed a coin, I won, and was then proved to be wrong in my route finding. There is no more miserable walking than through a young forestry plantation. The young pines scratched and tore our legs, we continually stumbled into deep wet-bottomed ditches, and clegs attacked us from every angle. Eventually, tired, thirsty, torn and scratched, we emerged from the trees and found the track. Jeff quietly cursed me under his breath.

It was easy going now, past the keeper's cottage at Kernsary, around the delightful loch of the same name, the magic of the place emphasized by a herd of several white horses grazing quietly by the track side. Dunlin purred and we heard the cry of a golden plover. Gulls wheeled over the still waters of the loch, and several anglers gently irritated us as they drank long draughts from cans of beer. That was just too much. With tongues hanging out like tired dogs, we stumbled into Poolewe, and straight into the post office-cum-store for cans of drink.

Since completing the walk, scenically the most varied I have enjoyed, others who have visited the area have told me that we were extremely lucky in our weather. We were blessed with the finest views in Scotland, and the memory of that walk will long remain with us as a reminder of what Scotland can be like when everything goes well. But the joy of that wilderness experience comes with a price. Years of stravaiging lesser hills in more accessible areas qualified Jeff and me for that walk. If you go to the Great Wilderness, make sure you have the experience behind you, or your memories may not be as happy as ours.

BACKPACKING GAELIC

A visitor to Scotland once coined this little rhyme:

A mountain's a mountain in England, but when
The climber's in Scotland it may be a Bheinn,
A Creag or a Meall, a Spidean, a Sgor,
A Carn or a Monadh, a Stuc or a Torr.

These lines actually serve to illustrate how precise the Gaelic language is. Whilst "mountain" covers all forms of terrain protuberances over a certain height (as opposed to a "hill"), the Gaelic actually specifies which type of mountain it refers to. *Ben*, or *Bheinn*, is a general term applied to mountains north of the border, but a *Sgurr*, for example, is a separate mountain, like a *bheinn* but more rocky. All the peaks in the Cuillin of Skye are Sgurrs. *Creag* means a rock, usually an outlying spur. A *Meall* is a lumpy sort of hill, and a *Monadh* is a flat-topped hill. *Tom* and *Torr* usually refer to low hills, whilst *Cnoc* will be fairly steep, but not the highest. *Maol* will be a bald bluff top, *Carn* will be high and certainly stony, and *Bidean, Bidein, Binnein, Stob, Sgurr, Stuc* and *Spidean* will always be bold mountains, often peaky or pinnacled.

A knowledge of these names can be a great help to the backpacker in Scotland, and can give one a good idea of what type of terrain lies ahead, besides being a constant source of interest and speculation. What dark and sinister events are commemorated in Coire Cath nam Fionn, the Corrie of the Battle of the Fingalians, or how did Loch Mhic Ghille-choile, the loch of the son of the thin man, get its name? Other names are descriptive: *Beag* means small, and *Mor* means big. Or perhaps the glens, bens or lochs are noted by their colour: *dubh* for black, *ban* for white or fair, *buidhe* for yellow and *ruadh* for red.

Pronunciation can be difficult, but don't be frightened to attempt it. Remember that "bh" and "mh" are pronounced or aspirated to "v" at the beginning of a word, for example,

Bhuiridh = Vooree, and *Mhadaidh* = Vatee. *-idh* at the end of a word, as you can see, is pronounced as "ee". "G" and "th" are pronounced hard, and "ch" is guttural as in "loch" (definitely not as in "lock"). "Fh" at the beginning of a word is silent, "ph" sounds as "f", and "sh" or "th" sounds "h".

There is no neuter in Gaelic, and the adjectives take the gender of the noun they qualify, "h" being inserted into the word to indicate the feminine. This changes the pronunciation of many words. For example, *mor* becomes *mhor* (pronounced "vor"). Other examples include: *Ban, bhan* (white) are pronounced "Ban" and "Van". *Beag* becomes *bheag* (pronounced "vegg"), *Buidhe* ("boo-ee") becomes *bhuidhe* ("voo-ee").

"An", or "the", is used before consonants except b, p and f, when it changes to *Am*. Before aspirates it changes to "a' ", for example, A'Mhaighdean, the Maiden. Before vowels and vowel sounds it changes to *an t-*, as in Coire an t-Sneachda (pronounced Corrie an trecht).

The following glossary is by no means exhaustive, but it should give you a rough idea of what many of the names mean, and how the more awkward ones are pronounced. Many place-names have been so corrupted from their original Gaelic or Norse that they are now unrecognizable or meaningless, and this is the great danger of trying to oversimplify the old names. Anglicizations, like Angels' Peak instead of Sgurr an Lochain Uaine, should be discouraged. How can anyone prefer Angels' Peak to the original Gaelic, which in any case means Peak of the Green Lochan and has nothing to do with angels.

EXPEDITION PLANNER

Route 1. Trans-Scotland Walk: Oban to Montrose.
Getting There. Oban is served by train from both Glasgow and Edinburgh.

Train Enquiries: Oban Railway Station, telephone number 0631 3083.

Montrose is also served by train from both Glasgow and Edinburgh.

Stores. Food can be purchased at Oban (also camping stores, gaz, etc.), Taynuilt, Bridge of Balgie (P.O. with limited stores), Tummel Bridge Campsite (also showers, restaurant, bar and good shop), Blair Atholl. Cairnwell (very limited), Glendoll Youth Hostel, Tannadice, Brechin. Food parcels can be sent to Blair Atholl railway station for collection *en route*.

Information. Tourist Information Office, Oban. 0631 3122/35551.

Route 2. Rathad nam Meirleach. Through Badenoch and Lochaber.

Getting There. Aviemore is on the Perth-Inverness rail line. Then taxi to Glenmore (Taxi stance, Aviemore 810205), 7 miles, or alternatively Highland Omnibuses run a bus service daily from the end of the ski season to the second Saturday in October. There are also daily bus services from mid December until the end of the ski season. Inquiries at Aviemore Bus Station, 0479 810658. There is also a bus from Aviemore to Fort William, Fridays only, and from Fort William to Aviemore, also Fridays only.

Stores. Food stores in Aviemore, Glenmore, Dalwhinnie, Fort William. Food parcels can be sent to railway station at Dalwhinnie for collection *en route*.

Information. Tourist Information Office, Aviemore; 0479 810363. Youth hostels at Aviemore, Loch Morlich, Kingussie, Loch Ossian and Fort William.

Route 3. Glen Nevis High-level Circuit.

Getting There. Fort William is on the West Highland railway line. In summer a bus runs up Glen Nevis daily to the lower falls at Polldubh. July and August only. Full details from Highland Omnibuses, 0397 2373.

Stores. Stores in Glen Nevis and Fort William. Mountaineering and camping supplies in Fort William.

Information. Tourist Information Office, Fort William, 0397 3582. Hill conditions and weather: Nevisport, Fort William; 0397 4921 and 4922.

Youth Hostel in Glen Nevis.

Route 4. Following the Gregorach.

Getting There. Postbus service from Callander. Connecting bus service to Glasgow and Edinburgh. Postbus leaves Callander Mon.-Sat. 07.45, arriving Trossachs 11.00. Mon.-Fri. 14.30, arriving Trossachs 14.57. Connects at Callander with W. Alexander & Sons (Midland) Ltd, for Stirling.

Stores. Food stores at Brig o'Turk and Strathyre.

Information. Youth Hostel at Lendrick, Trossachs Y.H. Phone Trossachs 227.

Route 5. The Knoydart Munros.

Getting There. There is no public transport along the north shore of Loch Arkaig. Private cars only. Alternatively, circular route can be followed from Inverie; ferry from Mallaig. Inquiries: Bruce Watt Cruises, 0678 2233. Mallaig is culmination point of West Highland Railway.

Stores. Only at Inverie (off route).

Information. Tourist Information Office, Mallaig, 0687 2170. No youth hostels in area.

Route 6. In the Footsteps of Montrose.

Getting There. Fort Augustus and Inverlochy are both on Highland Scottish Bus Co., Oban to Inverness route. Inquiries to Inverness Head Office, Seafield Road, Inverness. 0463 37575.

Stores. Food can be bought in Fort Augustus, Roybridge and Fort William.

Information. Tourist Information Office, Fort Augustus. 03203 6367.

Youth hostels at Loch Ness, Fort William (Glen Nevis).

Route 7. Trotternish in Skye.

Getting There. Bus from car ferry at Kyleakin to Portree. Bus from Portree to Kilmaluag (Duntulm Hotel). Information from Highland Scottish Bus Co., Park Road, Portree, Isle of Skye. 0478 2647.

Stores. Only in Portree.

Information. Information Centre, Meall House, Portree. 0487 2137.

Youth Hostels at Uig, Broadford and Kyle of Lochalsh.

Route 8. Comyn's Road.

Getting There. Both Blair Atholl and Kingussie (2 miles from Ruthven) are on the London-Inverness railway line.

Stores. Food can be bought in Blair Atholl and Kingussie. No stores *en route.* Carry all necessary provisions.

Information. Tourist Information Office, Kingussie, Invernes-shire. 05402 297.

Youth Hostels at Pitlochry and Kingussie.

Route 9. Over the Great Wilderness.

Getting There. Inverness-Ullapool bus connects with a Mon, and Sat. service from Braemore Junction to Dundonnell. In summer a bus runs from Poolewe to Dundonnell and back on Wednesdays. Leaves Poolewe 08.22 and 14.40. Information from M. Taylor, Westerbus, Badbea, Dundonnell, Wester Ross. No phone.

Stores. P.O. and store in Poolewe. Nothing *en route.* Carry all supplies.

Information. Gairloch, 0445, 2130.

No youth hostels. Nearest at Aultbea.

In addition to the above bus and train services, excellent services are provided by the Scottish Postbus Service. Enquiries to Scottish Postal Board, Operations Divisions (Postbuses), West Port House, 102 West Port, Edinburgh, EH3 9HS. 031-228 5241. Send for a copy of their Scottish Postbus Timetable. It can be invaluable in the more remote areas, and where trains and ordinary buses are infrequent. Another good guide is *Getting around the Highlands and Islands*, published by the Highlands and Islands Development Board, Bridge House, 27 Bank Street, Inverness, 1V1 1QR. 0463 34171.

GAELIC GLOSSARY

aber, abhair (avec) — river's mouth, occasionally a confluence

achadh (achay) — field, plain or meadow

aird — height, high point, promontory

airidh (airee) — shieling

allt — river or stream

amhalnn (avin) — river

aonach (anoch) — ridge

ath — ford

ban, bhan — white, bright, fair

beag — small

bealach (balloch) — pass, col or saddle

beith — birch tree

ben, benn, beinn — hill or mountain

bidean (bidjin) — peak

binnein — peak

bodach (podach) — old man

braigh (bray) — brae, hill top

breac — speckled

brochan — porridge

buachaille (boochal) — shepherd, herdsman, guardian

buidhe — yellow

buiridh — bellowing, roaring

cailleach (kay-lyac) — old woman

camas — bay

carn — cairn, hill, pile of stones

cas — steep

ceann — head

choinneach — mossy place, bog

chrois — cross or crossing place

ciche — pap

cill — cell or church

cioch — pap

ciste — chest, coffin

clach — stony

clachan — small village, township

chap, cnoc	hillock
coille	wood
coire, choire (corrie)	corrie, cwm
creachan	rock
creag	Crag, cliff
croit	croft
cruach, chruach	hill
cuach	cup, deep hollow
cul	back
curra	marsh, bog
dail	field
damh, daimh (damf)	stag
darach	oakwood
dearg (jerrag)	red, pink
diollaid	saddle
diridh (deeree)	a divide
dorus	strait, gate
drochaid	bridge
drum, druim	ridge
dubh (doo)	dark, black
dun	fort, stronghold
each	horse
eagach (ayach)	notched place
eas	waterfall
eighe (ay)	file, notched
eileach	rock
eilean or *eileni* (ie-lan)	island
eun	bird
fada, fhada	long
fearn	alder
fiadh	deer
fionn (fin)	white
frith	deer forest
fuar	cold
gabhar (gower)	goat
gaoth, gaaith (goo-ee)	wind
garbh (garv; garra)	rough
garbhanach	rough ridge
gartain	enclosed field

geal	white
gearanach	walled ridge
gearr	short
gille	young man, boy
glais	burn
glas, ghlas	grey or green
gleann	glen
glomach	chasm
gorm	blue
innis, inch	meadow, sometimes island
inver, inbhir	confluence
iolair	eagle
kin	head
knock, cnoc	hillock
kyle	strait
ladhar (lar)	forked, hoofed
lagan, lag	hollow
lairig (larig)	pass
laoight (loo-ee)	calf
laroch	dwelling place
leac	slab, stone
leathad	slope
leis	lee, leeward
leitir	slope
liath	grey
lochan	small loch
maighdean, mhaighdean (vy-a-jan)	maiden
mairg	rust coloured
mam	rounded hill
maol, mull	headland, bare hill
meadhon, mheadhoin (vane)	middle
meall (mell)	hill
moin, mhoin, moine	bog or moss
monadh (mona)	hill range, heathery hill
mor, mhor	big
muc, muice	pig
muileann, mhuilinn (violin)	mill
mullach	top summit

odhar (oor, our)	dun coloured
ord	*conical hill*
poite	pot
poll	pool, pit
puist	post
righ (rie)	king
ros, ross	promontory, moor
ruadh (roo-a)	red
rubha, rudha	point, promontory
ruigh	shieling
sail	heel
sean, sin	old
seileach	willow
sgeir	reef
sgiath	wing
sgurr, sgorr (sgoor)	peak, usually sharp pointed or rocky
sith	fairy
sithean	fairy hill
spidean	peak
sron	nose
stac	steep rock, cliff, sea stack
steall (steel)	waterfall
stob	peak
stuc	steap rock, peak
suidhe (soo-ee)	seat
tarmachan	ptarmigan
teallach (chellach)	forge, hearth
tigh	house
tir	area, region, land
tobar	well
tom	hill
torr	small hill
tulach, tulachan	hillock
uaine (oo-an)	green
uamh (oo-aa)	cave
uig	bay
uisge	water

INDEX